50 Reasons
Not To Have Kids

Joe Sindoni

ISBN 0-7414-3794-5

Published by:

INFIN∂ITY
PUBLISHING.COM

1094 New DeHaven Street, Suite 100
West Conshohocken, PA 19428-2713
Info@buybooksontheweb.com
www.buybooksontheweb.com
Toll-free (877) BUY BOOK
Local Phone (610) 941-9999
Fax (610) 941-9959

Printed in the United States of America

Printed on Recycled Paper

Published June 2007

<u>*Dedications*</u>

Gloria Jean — Your love, devotion, and encouragement made the publishing of this book a reality.

George — Your lifelong friendship, support and endless help has been a true blessing.

Lane — My friend through thick & thin. You are the brother I always wished I had.

Karen & Mindy — Thank you for your help and support when it was very much needed.

To all my Friends — Your loyalty is the foundation I've built my life upon.

This book is dedicated to my Godmother, Barbara DeMarco, for opening her heart to me and filling an enormous void in my life.

And to my sons, Joseph & Justin, who not only understood the reason for this book, but gave me an endless supply of material.

50 Reasons Not to Have Kids

Table of Contents

"The pressures of being a parent are equal to any pressure on earth. To be a conscious parent, and really look to that little being's mental and physical health, is a responsibility which most of us, including me, avoid most of the time because it's too hard. To put it loosely, the reason why kids are crazy is because nobody can face the responsibility of bringing them up."

John Lennon (1940-80), British rock musician, Founding Beatle, Stay at home Dad.

Introduction

I wish I had known this when I decided that having children was "just the thing to do." I believed it when Lennon said, *"All you need is love."* You do need love - lots of it! But you need much more.

The trials and tribulations with kids in this generation are unlike anything parents have had to deal with before. And, I'm not unlike most parents in being unprepared to handle it.

Teenagers today are angrier and more disconnected than my generation was. They view my generation with contempt, not just for living with, but for perpetuating the hypocrisy that we fought against when we were their age.

I grew up in the 1960's and 70's, so I know all about a "generation gap." I now know there is always a generation gap between parents and children. And there always will be.

It surprises me that such a *hip* group of parents, like we thought we were going to be, could be so out of touch with our children. But we are. And so will you.

After spending most of my adult life as a single dad, it feels like I've hit a wall. I never imagined myself as a single parent. But life is full of the unexpected. In fact, as a parent the only thing you can expect is the unexpected.

I could make my 18 year old get out into the world under the guise of "tough love." But, maybe if I had given him the tender love he needed in his early years, when just trying to make ends meet was where my time and energy was spent, I wouldn't have to be thinking about tough love now.

I took my children to counseling to fix them, only to discover that I needed fixing too. I didn't like that. But I was willing to be open to change.

Sure enough, many of the problems could be traced to what I was doing, or what I wasn't doing. And in many cases, what I never knew I should do.

School doesn't teach us about raising kids. We're taught the 3 R's in learning, not the 3 H's in parenting: heartache, heartbreak and heartburn.

And, I believe we are, and will continue to be, held more accountable than our parents were, both by society and our children. Forget about "do as I say, not as I do." It may have worked for your parents, but it will not work for you.

Our children are evolving as fast as our world is. They question more, know more, and demand more. And even though they need more, they often get less.

Unfortunately, we have made it socially acceptable to allow others to raise our children, by allowing strangers to care for them as early as a few months old.

We're not *really* willing to change our lives and make the major sacrifices that are essential in raising children, which will be pointed out in this book.

We have children expecting them to fill our hearts with love. But are we willing to fill our children's lives with our time?

Forget about this "quality time" B.S.. That's just a form of absolution for parents to ease the guilt. Children need both! Quality AND quantity. A baby should be expected to fill its diaper, not your heart.

Having a child in America today is viewed as a special gift that God, with his infinite wisdom, has bestowed upon us. Although we seldom let God, with his infinite wisdom, choose *when* or *if* we should have one.

Many forms of birth control are used to prevent pregnancy or terminate it when it happens. And if we don't receive this "*gift*," we use all kinds of artificial means to make it happen.

So much for God's infinite wisdom! The point is, making a baby is not a gift from God, any more so than a rainy day is. It's an instinctive and simple biological function that requires no skill or training.

All humans and animals can procreate. Even the lowest form of life instinctively procreates. God or nature, whichever you choose to believe, made it this way.

We have been given a mind with the ability to do the right thing, not just the instinctive thing. We can put thought, reason, and spiritual beliefs into our decision to procreate.

We should also consider potential risks for both the child and parents. And we must rationally evaluate our ability to provide physically, emotionally, and financially for the needs of a child for *at least* 18 years.

Having a child is viewed as something we all MUST do in order to have a fulfilling life. But a happy family which fills your inner needs exists only briefly, and is rarely as satisfying as in your imagination.

We often allow wonderful illusions of a joyful family life to overshadow reason and logic. This illusion makes it easy to ignore our own emotional emptiness, which will affect this child as surely as genetics will.

A happy family is like a mirage. You keep thinking you see it and struggle to attain it, but usually just find more hot sand. And if you do reach this oasis - drink up, savor it, because it will dry up quickly.

You'll quickly be back on your journey through a scorching, endless terrain of colic, teething, daycare, school, babysitters, broken bones, illness, disease, sex, drugs, alcohol, driving, disrespect, broken hearts, and all the unexpected things that an ever-changing life, in an ever-changing world, will bring.

During this heroic journey of parenthood, you can expect to carry the burdens, suffer through the setbacks and have your advice regularly ignored, only to be blamed for everything that goes wrong.

The many things you do will be unappreciated. You can easily be stretched beyond your tolerance. The unending stress often opens old emotional wounds that never healed properly.

Your child will be molded by your fears, unlived dreams, dysfunction and unhappiness.

Parents almost always dump their emotional pain onto their children. We hide it from co-workers and do our best to keep our friends from seeing it. But we pour it on our kids. Like a corrosive acid it continues to emotionally eat away at our children throughout their lives, and probably long after we're gone.

You can live *your* life to its potential by reaching for your own dreams, instead of creating another life to find them for you.

You can start a business, discover the artist within yourself, or choose a career that makes a positive difference in society. Be a mother or father to all children by being an advocate for children's issues, and making the world a better place for them to live.

This is *not* a book about how bad kids are. It's about how poorly prepared we are for the job of bringing them up. It dispels the myth that life with children is more fulfilling than a life without a child of your own.

Parents should be aware of the downside to having children. There's already plenty of voice to the upside.

Even if you still choose to have a child, this book can help. I've stepped in most of the parental bear traps along the journey of child rearing, my experiences may help you avoid some of them.

There's a Chinese proverb, *"A wise man learns from experience. A wiser man learns from the experience of others."*

50 Reasons Not To Have Kids comes from the trenches, not from a Ph.D. And who better to describe trench warfare (which parenting sometimes seems like) than someone who's been there. It may be the most honest book to offer some balance between choosing to, or choosing not to, have kids.

Making a baby is not a sacred event - raising a child is. *50 Reasons* is not simply a snapshot of the surface - it's a window into the soul of parenting.

"I wish either my father or my mother, or indeed both of them, as they were in duty both equally bound to it, had minded what they were about when they begot me."

Laurence Sterne (1713-68), Author.

Reason 1

To Save Your Marriage

"Maybe if we have a child. . .?" You may think it. You may say it. You may even believe it. Or, maybe you can't admit you're considering having a child to solve your marital problems.

Well, this is a good time to be honest, at least with yourself. If there are problems in your marriage, a child will just mask them temporarily — if at all.

What is it about having a baby that will make your marriage better? How is a baby going to accomplish this? What if it doesn't work, or the marriage gets worse, then what? The child suffers, that's what!

If children come into the world with the burden of saving a marriage — as many do — they sense it. When problems continue — as nearly all do — children try and fix them. When the marriage dissolves — as it likely will — children feel responsible for it.

Is it fair to put such a burden on a child - to bring a baby into a family with the expectation of healing those that are responsible for caring for it? It's a big load to put on such little shoulders.

Your marriage problems are not caused by being childless. And making a baby will not fix them. The problem is within you and your spouse. It has nothing to do with an innocent life.

1

Once you have a child, you will have even less time to work on these issues and more stress to compound them. And, you can add to that the hormonal changes that occur in many women during and after pregnancy.

Solving your problems is a job for a qualified therapist—someone trained to help couples fix their marriage.

Parents' love and commitment to each other should be secure *before* a child is conceived. A child needs to see and feel this from his or her earliest moments.

The relationship between a mother and father has a lifelong impact on a child. The most meaningful gift parents can give a child is to be in a healthy, loving relationship.

Work on building a strong marriage *first*. You'll be giving your child its best birthday present.

A child should be born into a loving environment - not expected to create it. A strong marriage can support a child - but a child can't support a weak marriage.

To comment on this or any **Reason** go to www.50reasons.com

"We say that a girl with her doll anticipates the mother. It is more true, perhaps, that most mothers are still but children with playthings."

F. H. Bradley (1846-1924), Philosopher.

Reason 2

Because Babies Are So Cute

The answer I often get when I ask the question: "Why do you want to have a baby?" is "because babies are so cute."

I don't hear this from guys. But surprisingly, I hear this as much from women in their 30's as I do from girls in their teens.

Puppies are cute, kittens are cute, squirrels and chipmunks are cute, so are baby elephants. But just because something is cute, doesn't mean you should rush to have one. What's little and cute today will be big and uncontrollable tomorrow.

For many women, going to stores, buying little clothes and dressing a baby is extremely pleasurable. This must be an outgrowth of a girl's childhood fantasy, because as a guy, even as a father, I don't get it.

Whether it's nature or nurture, little girls still love to play with baby dolls in their doll-house, while boys race sports cars on their Nintendo.

The problem is how easily a woman can turn her childhood fantasy into real life. At least a man needs a license and advanced training before he gets to drive a *real* race car.

Having been a single dad from the time my children were still in diapers, I spent a lot of time hanging out with moms. In my experience, the only thing that lights-up a woman's face more than seeing a baby, is a sweet-table at an Italian wedding.

Searching for my newborn son among the "babies on display" in the maternity ward, I quickly found out that not all babies are cute either.

Looking up and down the rows for my son, I started thinking: "I hope that's not mine," and "My God, look at the head on that one."

Then I see a scruffy little bald-headed one, and look up to read: "Boy Sindoni. "

Fortunately, babies do seem to get cuter with each passing day, but reality quickly sets in. There's nothing cute about a screaming baby in the food store or being thrown-up on. And that cute little two year old who's uncontrollable.., you can't take out the batteries.

You didn't just have a baby, you had a toddler and a teenager. A cute baby is oh so brief; a challenging child lasts a long time.

I'll admit that babies are *always* cute when they're sleeping. You'll stand there and gaze in their crib with wonderment at just how adorable this little child is.

With a warm feeling glowing in your heart, you'll retire to an evening of relaxation.., as he's climbing out of the crib.

And it just keeps getting cuter . . .

"Youth is quick in feeling but weak in judgment."

Homer (9th century B.C.)

Reason 3

You're Still a Child

It's not a good idea to *have* a child until you're finished *being* a child. Many people are still children, or still behave like children, well into their twenties.

Not that there's anything wrong with that; in fact it may actually be a good thing, especially for this generation.

If you're a young adult you were more than likely deprived of a childhood by being separated from your mother too soon, placed in daycare too young, and dumped into school too early.

Many parents are in big-time denial about this, but you'll know if it holds any truth for you.

Please don't confuse having *things* with having a childhood. In fact, the more *things* you had, the less childhood you likely had.

As parents, we tend to give *things* to compensate for not giving ourselves.

If, during your childhood, you had to deal with emotional traumas, such as your parents' separation or divorce, you can be sure that you missed a lot of your childhood.

I've seen these events shatter the lives of some very tough adults. As a child you didn't stand a chance, no matter how strong you tried to be.

Spending time between parents is not living *your* childhood, it's surviving the consequences of the unfortunate decisions the adults in your world made.

That you made the best of this situation is testament to the strength of your spirit. But it often leads to the unhealthy behavior of always making the best of bad situations, because it's what you expect.

It doesn't have to be this way. You don't have to create the bad situations in the first place.

There are some very unfortunate reasons why teenagers are having kids. A lot of it is society's refusal to acknowledge that your hormones are raging, even more so than those of adults.

Humans were created, by God or by evolution, to procreate at a young age.

When it comes to kids and sexuality, many parents take the ostrich approach of keeping their heads buried in ignorance, because of religion, lack of knowledge or sexual hang-ups. And you are left to discover your sexuality with little, if any, guidance.

This is not intended to make up for what your parents neglected to do, but it needs to be said. If you're having sex, use a condom or other method of birth control. Or keep it oral, which can be just as enjoyable, maybe more so, with no risk of pregnancy.

And let's not forget one of God's greatest gifts - masturbation. Do it to yourself, do it to each other, do it often - and enjoy it. You won't go blind! But having a baby, if you're not ready, will stunt your life.

If you didn't get to live your childhood, you're going to relive it at some point in your life, and I strongly encourage it when you're still young.

Your early adult years should be a time of discovery, fun, adventure, travel, and above all - freedom. A time to find out who you are.

These years are a great time to live *your* life, to enjoy your newfound independence. This is a time for a wide variety of experiences, tempered with a growing sense of responsibility. This is the soil where wisdom will begin to flower.

Use this budding wisdom — don't have a kid if you're still a kid.

"One can love a child, perhaps, more deeply than one can love another adult, but it is rash to assume that the child feels any love in return."

George Orwell (1903—1950) Author

Reason 4

No Matter How Much You Do, It Won't Be Enough

Parents are expected to make sure their children get all their childhood vaccinations, keep an accurate record, and see that all follow-up shots are received on the proper dates. And as a parent, you'll make sure it all gets done.

You're expected to get your children to the doctor when they're sick, pick up the medicine, know when they must take it, and make sure they do — whether it's bitter or sweet.

You're expected to register them for school, have all the paperwork done, and make sure they are up, dressed, fed and on time 5 days a week.

Paying for extracurricular activities and chauffeuring them back and forth will be expected as well. And you will do it all.

Hopefully these will be shared responsibilities. If they are, it will be difficult. If they're not, it will be impossible. But if you have to do the impossible for your child, you will.

You'll get used to making sure they wash their hands, brush their teeth and go to the dentist regularly, with them complaining all the way.

Year after year you'll host birthday parties, buy holiday presents, take them trick or treating, and plan all the other religious and holiday events.

You'll read bedtime stories, play games, spend countless hours doing homework, attending school functions, and taking an active part in their education.

Monitoring TV viewing, Internet use and music will be challenging, but you will do the best you can.

You will be aware of the everyday chores and responsibilities you are doing as well. Things like going to work, shopping, paying the bills, cooking the food and cleaning the house.

But don't expect *them* to be aware of it. It's a parent's job and it's expected.

Now the unexpected!

Your child comes home from school holding back their tears and tells you about an abusive situation. You call the principal and meet with the individual, who denies the behavior. You're angry and upset but defend your child.

Your child's grades start to slip and you get concerned. Maybe you get a tutor, maybe spend more of your own time, maybe both.

It doesn't help much, but you keep trying because you know what this means for your child's future. Your child struggles, you worry.

Your child is riding a bicycle and is hit by a car. You spend days visiting the hospital, weeks driving to physical therapy, hours of waiting, many sleepless nights and lots of tears. You do it all, and nurture your child back to health.

You catch your 12-year-old smoking a cigarette and spend countless hours lecturing about the dangers. It doesn't work. You try to scare him or her with the consequences, but the only person scared is you.

A party with alcohol gets raided by the cops and your child is arrested. You miss work, go to court and probably pay the fine.

Your child is frightened and you're upset. You give out consequences, which you have to enforce, and you do. But it happens again.

Your marriage is being strained by all the pressure of life. You realize how important two parents are, so you tough it out and stay together for the kid's sake. But nothing changes, except for the worse.

The relationship with your child has deteriorated to little more than regular yelling matches. You don't like your child's behavior, attitude or friends and feel responsible to fix or change them all. Try as you may, it doesn't work.

So you take your teenager to counseling to get help, only to discover that after all you've done, it's not enough. Your child needs more help and *you're* going to have to make some of the changes.

The situation doesn't improve and it seems as if you're the only one changing. Your kid gives up, but you keep trying.

You get a call at 1 AM from the hospital. Your child was in an automobile accident where alcohol and drugs were involved, and is in serious condition. Your heart drops and your insides shake. You've never felt this scared.

On the way to the hospital, memories flash through your mind. You see your child as an infant sleeping in your arms, the scared little tot on Santa's lap, and the happy youngster that tied his first shoelace.

You remember the proud look on your child's face, when you were given that special art project they did in school, as a gift. And you pray with all the shattered remains of your heart that your child doesn't die.

The joy you feel when you see your child alive and conscious quickly turns to anger. You're torn between wanting to hug him and tell him how much you love him, or scream at him for being so stupid and causing so much fear in your life. You end up doing both.

You seek out help, talk to family and friends, read the current literature and try anything you can to stop the destructive behavior. Your child resists everything you do.

The frustration is surpassed only by the love you feel. So you keep trying.

You sit down with your son or daughter and tell him or her that they have to go to a rehab. They kick and scream like you've never seen or heard before. But you stay strong and insist they have to go.

Your child calls you "a fucking ass-hole" right to your face. You're outraged as you drive to the rehab, and cry all the way home.

Your child is now 18 years old and has dropped out of school. The friends are the same, the attitude isn't much better, and the behavior is worse.

There's still a lot more help your child needs, and you can see it. But you just don't know how much more you're capable of doing, or how much more suffering you're willing to live with. Because you now know *no matter how much you do, it won't be enough.*

"They fuck you up, your mum and dad.
They may not mean to, but they do.
They fill you with the faults they had
And add some extra, just for you."

Philip Larkin (1922-1985), British poet.

Reason 5

You Were Raised in a Dysfunctional Family

Most of us grew up in dysfunctional families. The only real questions are what the primary dysfunction was and how severely it manifested itself.

Many families are riddled with dysfunction. But like living near a landfill, the stench becomes a part of your life.

"I had a great childhood, it was like a Disney family." I said that when I moved away from home at the age of 19. The sad thing is—I believed it because I didn't know any better.

Being shaken by my mother to the point of near death many times as a little child was normal for me. Being beaten by a rage-a-holic father while being called hateful and belittling things was normal.

I was poisoned with prejudice and a twisted set of values that justified whatever our family did. It was all "normal" for me.

I once saw a television interview of a mobster. He very candidly talked about how, while growing up, his family talked about "wackin" (killing) people while sitting around the dinner table. He said that he never gave it much thought, because it was normal behavior in his family.

12

One might think the dysfunction would be obvious in such severe cases. But unfortunately it's almost impossible for us to recognize the dysfunction we live in. It's what we were born into, and it's all we've ever known.

Any family where either parent abuses alcohol, food, drugs, themselves, their spouse or their children is dysfunctional.

Sometimes the less obvious dysfunctional behaviors, such as racial or religious prejudice, which are subtly instilled in many families, are the more insidious.

A mother who is aloof — who instead of shaking her child, withholds love and affection — can be just as damaging. The same is true of a father who is virtually nonexistent in his child's life.

It's difficult to see dysfunction in our lives. It is much easier to see it in others. Viewing other more seriously dysfunctional families makes us look OK. But we're kidding ourselves if we think, "Ours wasn't that bad, so therefore it didn't exist."

No matter how seemingly insignificant the dysfunction may seem, it will continue to grow as it is passed from generation to generation. Like a poisonous gas, it will slowly suffocate the happiness out of a family, but no one will see it.

A logical question is: Why should I look for trouble in my family? If *I'm* happy, then it's OK—why go digging?

You should look for dysfunction because you can be just as sure that you will pass on your emotional dysfunction, as your genetics, to your child.

In all likelihood, we know if our mother has breast cancer or our father has heart disease. It's easy to see and diagnose the physical. It's not easy to see the emotional, especially since we really don't want to, so we disregard it.

We may or may not be able to alter genetics, but we can definitely alter behavior. We can make a choice to tear off the blinders of denial and break the chain of dysfunction that may be very specific to our family and seem "normal."

Because we believe we survived the dysfunctional behavior of our family, it's easy to think it's not harmful - until it shows up in our children.

If we're unable to recognize it, it will be difficult to heal. Instead we're likely to feed the dysfunction and cause it to grow and manifest itself as pain and disharmony in the life and affairs of our children.

Dysfunctional behavior is a highly infectious disease that no medicine can cure. Unfortunately, in today's world when it shows up in our kids, drugs are often the first line of defense parents choose.

We are drugging our kids at an alarming rate. But a drug has about as much chance of fixing a dysfunctional family as butter has of fixing a diseased heart.

Denial is a blinding darkness that keeps us from seeing the faults in our own families. But it's vital that you take a good hard look at the family you grew up in before you decide to have kids.

Work on breaking the chain of dysfunction attached to you, so it won't shackle your children.

"Like many other women, I could not understand why every man who changed a diaper has felt impelled, in recent years, to write a book about it."

Barbara Ehrenreich (b. 1941), U.S. author, columnist.

Reason 6

Changing Diapers

Our friendly quoted author doesn't understand because she is not on this side of the testosterone barrier. There's some truth in the quote though.

Maybe not write a book, but men will brag about the *one* time we do change a diaper, and make it sound like we do it all the time. The truth is, a guy will do just about anything to get out of changing a diaper.

This must be one of those "Venus & Mars" things. Women don't seem to mind changing diapers as much as men do. Women actually sing lullabies while changing diapers. That requires breathing!

Moms still do the majority of the child-raising chores, especially in the early years. If you're going to become a mom, you're going to find out that when your husband does change a diaper, it's a momentous occasion — like when he remembers to put the toilet seat down.

But guys, you're still going to have to change some diapers. The pressure will be on for you to do your part.

Try as you may to put it off until your wife gets home (aiming the fan, putting the baby swing in another room), there will be times when the dreaded task is unavoidable. Sometimes you won't even be able to wait until halftime.

You're going to have to put your baby on a bassinet (baby work bench), open a soiled diaper (toxic waste site), and clean a messy, smelly butt - with no hazardous waste pay.

It's hard to imagine something that smells so bad can come out of such a cute little thing.

Maybe men just have sensitive noses. I mean we can tell if our clothes are clean with the "smell test."

When it comes to changing diapers, a mom will change too many, and for a dad, one is too many.

So I'll leave you with this dyslexic observation; *diaper* spelled backwards is *repaid*. And whatever side of the testosterone barrier you're on, that's what it is.

"Americans, indeed, often seem to be so overwhelmed by their children that they'll do anything for them except stay married to the co-producer."

Katharine Whitehorn (b. 1926), British journalist.

Reason 7

Divorce

Of course when you're thinking about having children, you're not thinking about breaking up. But over fifty percent of marriages will end in divorce. Statistically, that's a fact.

Divorce will be difficult on you, but even harder on your children, who will become helplessly stuck between two people they love and look up to. The more hurtful your divorce, the deeper the wounds will be in your child's life.

It's true that most children *survive* the experience, but at what cost? Divorce is one of the most painful experiences in an adult's life. But for children, it's torture.

As a single parent, you'll be lucky to squeeze in a few minutes a day for your own needs. Meanwhile, your responsibility to your children will increase.

Your economic situation will change - probably for the worst. You'll be left with an open wound, unique to divorce, that can be emotionally crippling. And the pain will bleed onto your children.

If you win custody, you will be thrust into a two-parent role, something no one parent can do.

Being a good parent is the most difficult and time-consuming job in the world. Being both parents is impossible.

You'll do your best, but your children will suffer. Your other half may be gone, but the cooking, cleaning, school affairs and, of course, your job or career are still there.

You'll be emotionally stretched to the limit, but nothing will let up, and you can't divorce yourself from your child.

Not by choice, but by lack of choice, you'll have far too little time to spend with your children. You will be too emotionally drained to provide the nurturing every child needs—and deserves.

Your stressed-out life will be dumped on your children—the ones least deserving of it.

The chances of developing an emotionally satisfying romantic relationship are slim. People without kids won't understand your needs, and those with kids won't have time for your needs.

Finding a person to accept your children is not easy, and even if *you* do find someone, your children will probably not accept them.

If you're the non-custodial parent, spending time with your children, even if the court orders "liberal visitation," will be difficult at best.

If another person enters the picture, you're going to have to deal with conflicting emotions that are buried deep within. It can rip your heart and soul to shreds.

With time, you can put your life back together. But what's left is the tattered remains of the person you once were. What will be left of your child will be the tattered remains of the person they could have been.

Divorce is damaging enough without children. With children, it's life shattering.

"Motherhood is the strangest thing, it can be like being one's own Trojan horse."

Rebecca West(1882-1983) Author

Reason 8

2 A.M. Feedings

Do you think you get enough sleep? Studies show that most of us are not getting enough sleep, and living high stress lives — as if we needed studies to tell us this.

Well, if you have a child, you can add other interruptions to your sleep.

The day after you have a baby, your life will be exactly the same as it was the day before. Except, physically and emotionally, you have added the equivalent of starting a business AND beginning your first year in a new school.

And ladies, while guys talk a good story about helping out, we really just talk a *lot* about the *little* we do. You'll be getting up most of the time for diaper changing and feeding, even if you're not nursing.

You may be dismissing this reason because it only lasts a short time. But nothing ever seems to last a short time with kids—except the time you spend together. One thing just gets replaced with something else.

2 A.M. feedings turn into 2 A.M. panic attacks when your teenager isn't home, hasn't called, and you KNOW that something is terribly wrong. You'll try to think rationally, but your rational thinking will tell you something bad MUST have happened.

This sleep interruption is pretty much gender neutral, although moms do seem to lose more sleep worrying.

Then there is the 2 A.M. call from the police. This is far more frequent now than in past generations. All I can tell you about this is: it usually involves alcohol, and it's unlikely something terrible happened to your child.

It's usually, "we've got your son, he's being charged with underage drinking," or "we have your daughter, she was at a party where there was alcohol."

But you still experience dreadful fear, followed by equally felt anger at your child, and another sleepless night.

You'll think back to the blissful days of 2 A.M. feedings.

Once you have a child, you can say good night to a good night's sleep!

"If you bungle raising your children, I don't think whatever else you do well matters very much."

Jacqueline Kennedy, (1929-1994) U.S. First Lady.

Reason 9

You Don't Have The Time

Children, from the moment they're born, want your time, demand your time, and deserve your time. It doesn't take very long (about six months) before it becomes impossible to keep up with the demand.

You only have seventeen and a half more years to go.

Over the course of the past century, we've created hundreds of products to free up time for ourselves. Every conceivable "time saving" appliance has been invented. Technology now lets us do just about anything from our phone or computer.

Still, it's necessary to have a 24-hour society, because we just don't have enough time to get things done.

Do you think the holidays are stressful now? When you have a child, you become Santa Clause, the Tooth Fairy, the Easter Bunny and a host of other characters, all requiring more of your time.

And you can add to your schedule: birthday parties, school plays and special events as well.

It's ironic that we spend so much time doing things for our kids, but so little time doing things with them.

Parents often try to drown their feeling of guilt by flooding their children with things. But there's nothing we can buy for their room that can replace the time we don't spend in their life.

Where are *you* going to get the time for these additional responsibilities?

You may be thinking "I'll just make time." But only Julius Caesar was able to do that. What you'll do is cram more things into the little time you have.

This creates a very stressful condition that takes its toll over time. Unfortunately, children feel the effect almost immediately, as the stress of your busy world spills into your kid's life.

All of your emotions, good and bad, are absorbed by your children. Unfortunately, we can't bury our emotions any more than we can dig up more time.

Children need lots of our time! The parent propaganda about "*quality time*" is exactly that. Parents often hide behind *quality* time because they know they're not spending *enough* time.

Do you have enough time to do the things you want to do? Is there enough time in your day to do the things you have to do? Do you have the time to take care of your own needs? Because if you don't have the time for yourself, you don't have the time for a child.

"Of all the animals, the boy is the most unmanageable."
Plato (427-347 B.C.), Greek philosopher.

Reason 10

It Might Be A Boy

When my wife was pregnant with our first child, I was often asked if I wanted a boy or girl. I would usually say the standard answer, "I don't care as long as it's healthy."

But I really wanted a boy. I don't know why I wanted a boy – I just did. You think I might have known better, after all - I am one.

Boys have something running through their veins pushing them into all kinds of trouble. I'm sure it has something to do with our early evolution, but it wreaks havoc in today's world.

It's called testosterone! From infancy, testosterone pushes boys into high-risk behavior.

A boy will climb out of the crib, fall and get hurt, but keep right on doing it. When he gets his first tool set, it's just a matter of time before he bops his sister with the hammer.

She may have antagonized him, but he is the one who will get in trouble. Ironically, he'll learn a valuable lesson: in conflicts with girls, the boy usually losses.

When your son starts school he has to deal with other testosterone beings. Bullying, intimidation and fights are likely to greet him early on.

There's a dominance thing that starts early in life. Boys have to navigate between the competing forces of: fear and courage, right and wrong, fitting in or being left out.

If you have a sensitive boy, it can be more challenging. There is nothing more upsetting than your son coming home crying and humiliated after being in a fight.

We have a tendency to just blow-it-off and say, "All boys go through it." Yes they do, but some never get through it. For many, the wounds remain unhealed. Childhood negative experiences often mold the adult.

In school your son will often get into trouble for doing boy things, not bad things. And teachers are more likely to say that your son should be put on medication.

Your son won't be satisfied to just skate on a skateboard, he'll build ramps to jump over things. He will go a lot faster on his sled, take more risks with his bicycle, and often use his body as a battering-ram.

As boys get older they continue to be more willing to engage in high-risk behavior. Boys think they're indestructible. But the results will be more broken bones, more stitches and many more skinned elbows and knees.

Tantrums during the "terrible twos" will become happy memories compared to what testosterone will be like in the teenager years.

Your son will most likely drink alcohol. Alcohol advertising is pervasive and it's linked to everything boys find cool—from sports to rock concerts. That it's illegal for teenagers plays right into the hands of testosterone, which naturally pushes boys to take risks.

Then comes the dreaded moment when your son begins to drive. Testosterone and vehicles are a deadly combination.

Your son will be far more likely than your daughter to drive fast and take chances with a car. Boys love the power of an automobile, and your son is going to find out just how much power it has.

Add alcohol to the mix, and it's almost certain that an accident will happen.

I watched my sons go from one high-risk behavior to another. And I saw the tragedies mounting among the boys in our community.

A boy who went to their high school overdosed on drugs and died. A car full of boys crashed and some of their friends ended up in critical condition.

I watched them grieve when a boy their own age, who went to the rival Catholic High School, was killed in a car crash while driving drunk.

Unfortunately, these tragedies are the only things that will have an impact on your son. And you can do little more than pray that he isn't one of the examples.

And in many of our cities, the risks boys encounter begin shortly after the umbilical cord is cut. Violence, gangs, and guns are as much a part of a boy's life as bicycles, baseball, and basketball.

If there are guardian angels, boys keep them working overtime. It's not the devil that makes them do it, it's testosterone.

We live in a high-risk world, and boys are high-risk creatures. The only thing scarier is: Having a girl! That's next.

"My daughter -- our daughters -- are in big trouble, and we're not talking about it. I'm talking serious trouble. robbery, shoplifting, drugs, babies."

Leonard Pitts Jr., Columnist

Reason 11

It Might Be A Girl

Yes my friends, the quote above is a very telling and frightening opinion, not just from a columnist, but from a father with two daughters.

When I tell parents with daughters that I have sons, I often hear, "you're lucky" or "girls are more difficult."

Knowing how challenging boys are, it's easy not to believe them, but I've heard it said too often and too passionately to dismiss.

When I was growing up in the 1970's, boys got into most of the trouble, and were far more reckless than girls. Although girls did some mildly bad things, they were not to the same extent and certainly not to the same degree.

This has all changed. Just go visit juvenile court and see the inroads girls have made into this once male-dominated venue.

Girls today are even fighting like boys. They may even be fighting more often than boys. It's scary to know this and very ugly to see.

The most visible form of self-abuse can be seen with the number of girls who are smoking. It seems that almost every high school girl I see is smoking a cigarette, even though we thoroughly educated this generation about the dangers.

Have you noticed that tattooing is more popular today than ever with girls? Well, it is.

How about body piercing? Girls are not just piercing their ears, they're piercing their noses, eyes, cheeks, tongues and even their private parts — and not just one. I've seen faces with ten or more pieces of metal sticking through them.

And there's another trend gaining popularity — branding. That's right, what gets done to a cow.

This is not a statement. Dying your hair purple is a statement. This is body mutilation.

They're either screaming out in pain, or for attention — but they're screaming pretty loudly.

This is the world that your daughter is going to grow up in. And it's getting worse.

Girls are drinking alcohol right up there with the boys today. And since boys and girls usually drink together, let's look at what we know about this situation.

Boys get more aggressive, and girls get more sexually permissive. That's like gasoline and a lit match.

A boy will wake up with a physical hangover, but your daughter will likely suffer a reputation hangover, which will last a lot longer.

I thought my generation put an end to the sexual double standard. We certainly did for ourselves.

But we obviously didn't pass what we learned on to our children, because there is still a reputation thing: Good for boys, bad for girls.

In addition girls suffer with eating disorders far more often than boys. If low self esteem were a disease, it would be epidemic among our daughters.

And from this is built a life of bad decisions, self

27

abuse, attempts at finding love to heal themselves, willingness to be abused by others, and going from one dysfunctional relationship to another.

Finally, girls are harmed even more than boys when their parents get divorced. The mother will likely get custody, and this will critically damage the role that a father MUST play in a girl's life.

There's a big difference between a girl having a father, and having a father who lives at home.

Every time I hear of a girl getting in trouble I ask my sons if her father is living at home.

The answer is overwhelmingly - No.

When I hear boys talking about a girl with a "reputation," it's the same thing — no father at home.

A girl without a father is a girl who is always searching for one.

This often leads to our daughters getting pregnant by a guy who you probably wouldn't trust with your trash removal. He's going to be entrusted with your daughter's emotions and the life of a child – your grandchild.

Our quoted columnist also related this: "*Makes you wonder, what has gone wrong with our girls? I once asked a policeman about it, asked him if I was just imagining things. He said no. And he said this: Out of 10 runaways he was chasing at that time, nine were teenage girls. So many girls trying to escape their own lives.*"

And these troubled behaviors cross all social and economic barriers. These behaviors are prevalent - whether rich, poor, or struggling somewhere in between.

What once was sugar, spice and everything nice, is now cigarettes, sex and everything complex.

"Selfishness is not living as one wishes to live, it is asking others to live as one wishes to live."

Oscar Wilde (1854-1900), Playwright, author.

Reason 12

To Take Care Of You When You Get Old

It's been enlightening talking to people during the writing of this book. One of the most surprising things I discovered was how some very unselfish people had some surprisingly selfish reasons for having kids.

One of the more common reasons stated was, "to have someone take care of us when we get old."

Historically, parents believed they were giving the "gift of life" to their children. As a result, they felt that children owed a life of servitude to their parents.

This underlying belief still exists today, but it's as incorrect as the belief that the earth is flat, and just as outdated.

We do not give the gift of life to our children. God or nature does. So they don't *owe* us anything.

A more enlightened belief may be that the gift of life is given to *us* as parents.

Knowing that the time spent caring for *you*, as an elder parent, is often going to necessitate neglecting *their* family's needs, isn't it unfair to take advantage of our children's sense of loyalty?

Their primary responsibly should be for the needs of their children and spouse at that time in their life.

A parent's concern should always be for their children, no matter what age. That concern must include their life as a wife or husband, and most especially as a mother or father.

We need to realize this when we are making the choice to bring a child into this world. Our responsibility is always to those we brought into this world, not the other way around.

The needs of our children can easily be pushed aside when it comes to caring for our parents. Many parents expect their adult children to be full time caregivers for them, and often use sympathy and guilt to get their way.

This form of coercion often causes stress and dissension within a family. There's nothing wrong with adult children helping their parents, but often that help becomes all consuming, and causes undue hardship on an upstarting family.

If you're going to have children, it's equally important that you don't allow your parents to adversely affect your time with your family—children and spouse, as it is that you don't someday do it to your children.

Our parents may not understand the stress, demands, and pressures of raising a family in today's world, and often monopolize and manipulate our lives.

I've seen elder parents put their children through enormous stress, and even cause dissension among brothers and sisters, because of their unwillingness to live in an assisted living facility. And they compound the stress by expecting their care to come from their children.

Will your parents do this to you? Will you do this to your children?

Having lived in Florida, I've seen how communities that cater to the needs of the elderly not only make living easier and better managed, but make them feel younger, and enjoy a full life, right up to the end.

I've witnessed how helpful and understanding the old folks are to one another, because they can relate to the needs, requirements and sufferings that are unique to advanced age.

I've seen the same in other well run assisted living facilities outside of Florida. The question is not whether an enjoyable and productive living environment can be created for our aging parents, and for ourselves some day, but how we can expand the good facilities, and close down the bad ones.

As a society, we spend an enormous amount of money on hospital stays and medicine, but nowhere near enough on happy living and productive and meaningful activities for the elderly.

Happy = Healthy. Active = Alive.

We should advocate this for our parents, and for ourselves when the day comes.

And I can't help but wonder if this generation of kids will have much concern at all about putting their parents in assisted living facilities.

After all, this is a generation of children who were placed in daycare when they needed us most, deprived of the time, attention, and love that is vital in the early years of life, and can only come from a parent.

This daycare trend is likely to continue.

If we won't sacrifice for our children during their most tender years, why should we expect them to sacrifice for us during our most fragile years?

Having children to take care of us when we get old is a selfish act. Instead put the money you would spend on raising a child into an IRA (Individual Retirement Account), and you'll go out in style.

I think a fitting alteration to the famous quote from President John F. Kennedy can sum it up best, "Ask not what your children can do for you—ask what you can do for your children."

"The law is a sort of hocus-pocus science, that smiles in yer face while it picks yer pocket."

Charles Macklin (1690-1797), Irish actor, dramatist

Reason 13

The Parent Tax

We have a government that does one thing extremely well — take money from its people! If there is a way to bleed money from us, the government will find it.

But taxing parents for having kids? The government could never do that and get away with it, one might think.

Well, maybe not directly, but most of what we pay in taxes is indirect, hidden, or attached to something else. Few governments pass up the opportunity to get more money from their people. Ours is no exception, even though the birth of this government came from the unfairness of taxes.

Your kid: cuts school — you pay a fine; gets caught smoking — court, and BIG fine; sneaks into the skating rink — court, and fine. If they hang out with their friends on a corner — court, and fine. Use a skateboard (illegal in many towns) — court, and fine.

These fines are taxes, as real as what is taken from your paycheck or hidden in a gallon of gas. Your crime—having a kid. Your child's crime—behaving like a kid.

Kids do things wrong—always have, always will. That's what kids are supposed to do. That's how they learn. That's what childhood not only allows, but provides as nature's way of teaching and learning.

A group of kids sneak into the local swimming pool and are caught by the cops. Do the police bring the kids home, feel good that they may have saved them from drowning, and let the parents handle it?

Nope! One more thing to do, collect the tax. "Please sign here Mr. Sindoni, this says we apprehended your son. . ."

Of course, what the citation says is: loitering and prowling and a few other charges piled on.

Court and fine!

A variety of offenses once brought only a scolding, or detention after school. Today, those same offenses mean a day's lost work for parents to go to court, and a tax levied on the family in the form of a fine and court costs.

Too many minor things have become criminal for this generation of kids, and it's getting worse.

Your kid goes to a party where there's drinking, and it's raided by the cops. You're child IS NOT drinking, but that doesn't matter—he was there.

You miss another day's work, another day's pay, and likely get fined on top of it.

When confronted with overzealousness, unfairness, and blatant interference with what has historically been parent/child issues, you are often as angry with the system as you are with your child.

When I was growing up, the police would take your beer and pour it out right in front of you. They made you stand and watch as punishment.

Or worse, they hauled you into the police station and called your parents. Then you had to see your parents' disappointment and face their wrath. But no citation.

Today parents are being fined for the crime of being parents and our children are being used as hostages. If you fall behind on paying your fine, you'll get a notice stating that your child is going to be arrested.

Whether there's a conscious effort in place to raise revenue in this way is not relevant. The fact is, it's happening.

The process it puts parents through is confusing, time consuming, and stressful. Certified letters come in the mail, often harshly worded and intimidating.

It's never pleasant getting these types of notices, especially when they come from the courts. It makes you feel like a bad person and a bad parent.

It doesn't matter if you're a two-parent working family, or a single parent struggling to pay your bills. It doesn't matter that you're attending parenting classes and getting counseling for your child—rarely covered by insurance. You'll miss a day's work and will most likely be fined as well.

For what? For having kids who are doing what kids have been doing since before the time of Jesus—making bad decisions.

The children with the most problems are often in the families with the most financial hardship. Many are single-parent families.

The most harmful thing that can happen to a family struggling to stay afloat, is to load on more financial weight.

A fine is always an inequitable and unfair punishment.

If you're rich it's not a hardship or punishment. But if you're poor, your child will likely end up in a detention center or jail.

If you're in the middle, it takes food off the table, or prevents you from getting the constructive help your family needs.

As of this writing, the mood in America is to get even tougher on kids. That will mean an even higher Parent Tax by the time your child reaches the troubling middle and high school years.

Don't you already pay enough taxes?

"Never lend your car to anyone to whom you have given birth."

Erma Bombeck (b. 1927), Journalist, author.

Reason 14

Driving

Driving is something that I have mixed emotions about.

The adolescent advocate in me says kids should be allowed to drive at around 16 years old. The parent in me says they shouldn't be allowed to drive until they're 25.

That's about the age when high risk taking begins to decline, and maturity begins to influence actions and decisions.

By the time your kids are 16 years old, you could have circled the globe with all the miles you will have logged as their chauffeur.

There's a part of you that will welcome the freedom from being an unpaid taxi driver. But you'll quickly realize it's a bad trade off.

Reality sets in as soon as you call your insurance company to add your child to the policy. Your rate goes up - way up!

Yes, you can make your kid pay his own insurance, but that's just one of those family illusions. You're responsible for the financial needs of your child, even if they're working.

What they spend on car insurance, they can't spend on clothes or college. So guess who's gonna pay for those?

But this is just the beginning.

Once your child gets a license, your car will be driven a lot more, and get beat-up a lot faster. Considering that a car is likely to be your second biggest investment, behind a house, this should not be taken lightly.

In one year a kid can put two years of mileage and four years of wear and tear on your car. And with college just around the corner, a new car or added auto repair bills can be a big problem.

Kids by their very nature are more reckless than adults. They're less able to grasp the full magnitude of risk associated with driving, and more likely to put themselves in situations that could cause serious injury or death.

Luck, or the good graces of God, will come into play more than you would like to know once your kid starts driving.

You can almost expect that your car will be in an accident. Hopefully it will just be the car that's damaged. But even so, we all know what that means.

Car in the shop, higher insurance rates—*again*, and a good chance of a lawsuit. Even a fender-bender is like a bad visit to the dentist.

And now the most serious issue: According to the U.S. Bureau of Transportation Statistics, the #1 cause of death for kids 15 through 24 is automobile accidents.

On average, 340 kids this age are killed in automobile accidents **every day**. I suspect the number of kids being paralyzed is equally as high.

You may have a responsible child, but once he or she reaches the driving age, their life becomes far more mobile, and far more dangerous—even if they don't have a driver's license or their own car.

Many of their friends will be driving and your child will be riding with them. Who knows how good that kid can drive? Who knows what drugs he or she is on?

And I'm not talking just illegal drugs. We're drugging our kids for everything from a runny nose to not sitting still in school.

These are drugs! And can be just as impairing as illegal drugs with alertness and reaction.

Our politicians have not addressed the problems surrounding driving in this country. They just don't want to tackle the issue of too many cars on the road and too many unqualified drivers.

I suspect that campaign contributions and other influences by affected industries and bureaucracies have something to do with this.

How else can one explain that so little attention is devoted to one of the single biggest killers of people—driving.

We could start by giving a test that is an actual indication of whether someone can drive. What we do today is the equivalent of watching someone doggy paddle in the kiddy pool, and then dropping them in the ocean.

We need to implement a test that requires real driving and involves real life situations.

For young and old alike, if you can't drive, YOU CAN'T DRIVE. Period!

This will be a good motivation to rebuild our public transportation, which is in desperate need of renovation.

Altering our reliance on the automobile can be done with little inconvenience. And in the entrepreneurial spirit of this country, businesses will emerge to fill the need, and do it more creatively than we could ever imagine.

If you think a Sunday spent watching your favorite sport's team lose is nerve-racking, wait until you spend it teaching your child to drive.

Sunday is the day many parents take their kids out driving because it's the only day when the traffic isn't insane. Or maybe it's because many of us feel closer to God on this day.

Either way, you'll question the sanity of letting teenagers drive, and you'll need the patience of a saint to be their driving instructor. You may miss Sunday church, but you will still be praying.

"As to the family, I have never understood how that fits in with the other ideals-or, indeed, why it should be an ideal at all. A group of closely related persons living under one roof; it is a convenience, often a necessity, sometimes a pleasure, sometimes the reverse; but who first exalted it as admirable, an almost religious ideal?"

Rose Macaulay (1881-1958), Novelist, essayist.

Reason 15

The Loss of Freedom

In your life before children, going out to dinner or to a movie is enjoyable, but it's no big deal. Going to a ball game, shopping or to the local pub is probably something you casually do whenever the spirit moves you.

That's because you still retained some personal freedom.

After you have children, going to dinner and a movie will be a *glorious* occasion. It will be so exciting that you'll spend half the night just talking about the fact that you're out. And you'll spend the other half of the night talking about the kids or worrying if they're alright.

Once you have children, everything will have to be planed in advance. If you enjoy the freedom of being able to have sex in the kitchen or on the living room couch - forget it!

Many of the little things in life that you take for granted before you have kids will become cherished and infrequent events. Unless you're wealthy enough to have a maid and a nanny, you can forget about your own personal time.

The freedom that you once had to do things spontaneously, will spontaneously combust.

It's not like we have a lot of freedom to begin with. Look at all the responsibilities you have on a daily basis, and how often they prevent you from doing the things you want to do with your life.

Now add a child to the picture. Whatever life doesn't demand from you physically, mentally and emotionally, your child will.

One parent will likely give up the majority of his or her freedom to raise the child. Children are extremely demanding from the moment they're born. They have lots of needs that you're going to have to provide for.

If personal freedom is something you value, it will become priceless, and virtually unattainable.

Whatever amount of involvement you have bringing up your child, your choices still must be made with your child's future in mind—not yours.

The goals, dreams and desires you had must now take a back seat to those of the child you brought into this world. Your goals are no longer as important as your child's grades.

As you surrender your desires, you sacrifice yourself. The pursuit of your own destiny is a noble purpose in life — maybe the most noble purpose. But your dreams will be obscured by the demands of raising a child.

You don't need to have a child to be active in a child's life. Instead of having your own kids, consider getting involved with children in your neighborhood. Kids need all the positive input from adults they can get.

Become an advocate for children's rights. You'll be loved, respected and admired by the kids you help. And you'll keep what little freedom you still have.

"They talk so beautifully about work and having a family and a home.., but it's all worry and head-aches and respectable poverty."

Wallace Stevens (1879-1955), Poet.

Reason 16

You Can't Afford To

Having and raising a child cost a lot of money. According to a report by the Department of Agriculture it will cost about $150,00.00 to raise one child to the age of 17 — but I'd swear I've spent more than that just feeding my sons.

I don't know why they chose to stop there. I can assure you that some big expenses will come after the age of 17.

According to that government figure, your child is going to cost you almost $9,000.00 a year. Is your employer going to increase your pay? Are you going to get a second or third job?

If so, how are you going to find the time for your child? Are both parents going to work? Who will then care for your most precious possession—your child? And how much will that cost?

This is all your responsibility if you're going to become a parent.

That government figure didn't factor in things like college or trade school. And then there are the other things that parents do, like helping your children get their first car, or a down payment on a home, or the cost of a wedding. Big expenses!

It's human nature to want our kids to have a better life than we had. This often puts us on a financial treadmill that leads to overworking, over spending, and over extending our credit. Many families are left with debt for years after their children are gone, and many end up in bankruptcy.

There are more serious things that also need to be considered. Studies show that poorer children generally score lower on IQ tests. This is most likely due to inadequate prenatal care and poor nutrition, which is most likely a result of not having enough money or adequate insurance—which is epidemic today.

And once a child is born, it's likely that illnesses will be improperly treated.

Then there's dental care which is one of the more expensive and easily neglected needs of our children. These things will affect your child for life.

Many people have children without even taking the time to develop a basic financial plan. More planning is put into buying a car or opening a business than is put into starting a family.

Financial considerations must be a part of family planning — not just how many kids you will have.

One Hundred Fifty Thousand Dollars!! This could be enough for you to take a cruise around the world, or have a little less financial stress in your life, and a little more of life's pleasures as you get older.

Before you bring a baby into your life, answer this question: Can you afford to?

"Conformity is the jailer of freedom and the enemy of growth."

John F. Kennedy (1917-63), U.S. President.

Reason 17

It's The Thing To Do

Get married and have a couple of kids, "it's the thing to do." It's easy to casually accept this well worn practice, or underestimate the compelling force that it is. But underestimating it can get you into deep water.

We are conditioned to do what is expected of us. When we comply, there are emotional and physical rewards; when we don't, there are usually negative consequences. This type of coercion affects us on both conscious and unconscious levels and continues throughout our lives.

Parents insist on conformity from birth — then school takes over. As adolescents, we may have revolted with what we did with our hair or the music we listened to, but deep within us the foundation was being laid for conformity.

Then it's out into the working world and more conformity. Even in our nonconformity—dress down Fridays—we conform. It's such a part of our lives that we don't realize how powerful the influence is.

The force to conform sweeps us away like a mighty ocean current. And since everyone else is being swept in the same direction, we feel safe.

Family and friends are often the ones who push us into this sea of conformity, with questions that assume things like: *When* are you going to start a family? *How many* children do you want?

These questions have a bigger effect on us than we may like to admit.

Take a closer look at who puts the pressure on you to have children. It's your friends with kids. They've done it, now they want you to do it. Conformity loves companionship.

Unfortunately, you're not going to get the whole truth from those who have kids. Rarely will they tell the depth of the bad experiences, or maybe they haven't faced them yet.

It's not intentional lying. It's human nature to want those close to us to do like we've done. It gives us a sense of security.

Wisdom would have us take a closer look at this powerful current that sweeps so many away. Don't just take a peek on a calm day when everything looks smooth. Check it out when it's rough.

Take a friend's child into *your* home for a day or two, or better yet - a week or two. Every parent needs a break. Your friends could use one and you can experience for yourself how strong an undertow you can handle before you dive in.

Look at it like swimming in front of a lifeguard. If you get into trouble, you can be rescued. But when they're your children, it's sink or swim.

As adults, we should realize that it's not always good doing something just because it's expected. "It's the thing to do" is not a good reason to start a family.

The fact that so many are jumping in doesn't mean you have to take the plunge. You can remove yourself from the sea of conformity and make your own waves.

When it comes to having children, "the thing to do" is **not** the thing to do.

"There are times when parenthood seems nothing but feeding the mouth that bites you."

Peter De Vries (b. 1910), Author.

Reason 18

Colic

This may be your earliest test as a new parent. There's a lot of speculation as to what colic is and what causes it. However there is no real cure, at least not medically.

What is known about colic is: it's a condition of early infancy that results in severe abdominal pain and is marked by chronic irritability and crying. Colic usually goes away by the sixth month of age, but if it happens to your child, it will feel like an eternity.

It's not unusual for a baby with colic to cry from 9PM until the early morning hours. This can happen almost every night. This inconsolable crying will tear your heart to shreds. You will try everything, but nothing will work.

If you're young, struggling financially, in an unstable relationship, or just physically overworked, you already have enough pressure in your life. Add a colicky baby and the situation may become more stressful than you can handle.

Feelings of sympathy, fear, frustration and helplessness can lead to depression and even anger. The combination of exhaustion and exasperation will try your tolerance.

When emotions get stretched to the limit, it's not only possible for you to snap, it's likely. Unfortunately, it's often the suffering infant that we snap on.

If you're in a violent or aggressive relationship or you grew up in a home where beating, whipping or other physical abuse was the common form of discipline, you will likely respond to your child's suffering with aggression.

Even a single outburst can have devastating results.

Colic is believed to be the major cause of Shaken Baby Syndrome. It's also suspected that colic is a major reason so many child-abuse cases involve infants under six months old.

In addition to potentially deadly consequences for the child, this aggression can have serious ramifications for the parents. Society no longer tolerates violent acts against children. What may have been overlooked in the past, will put you in jail today.

According the American Academy of Pediatrics, about one in five babies will develop colic. If that one is *your* child, will you have the patience and temperament to handle it?

"Come mothers and fathers
Throughout the land
And don't criticize
What you can't understand
Your sons and your daughters
Are beyond your command."

Bob Dylan (b1941), Singer, songwriter.

Reason 19

Your Parents Want Grandchildren

Maybe it's because they can enjoy them, or spoil them, or make up for all they did wrong with their own children, but parents often have an overwhelming yearning for grandchildren.

Many people choosing to be childfree are feeling pressure from their parents to give them grandchildren. I don't know if this was ever a good reason to have children, but it clearly isn't today. *"The Times They Are A Changin."*

The world you'll be bringing your children into is not the same world you were born into. Your parents may be well-meaning, but they don't have a clue about the challenges of parenting today. Their parenting experiences are about as relevant now as a manual typewriter.

You already spent the better part of your life doing what your parents wanted, or what pleased them. You don't owe them grandchildren.

At some point all children must cut the umbilical cord, and live life nourished by their own needs and desires instead of those of their parents.

As parents get older they start behaving like children anyway. Maybe it's their way of getting back at us, by acting as irrational as we did as kids. An older parent can be just as stubborn and challenging as any two year-old.

Parents want grandchildren. It's an opportunity to do the things they wish they had done with their own children. And it's a compelling reason to want grandchildren, but it's your parents' reason, not yours.

You can do yourself and your parents a bigger favor by taking some of that $150,00.00 it costs to raise a child, and help them buy a nice condo in Florida instead.

"Education is what remains after one has forgotten everything he learned in school."

Albert Einstein (1879-1955), Theoretical physicist.

Reason 20

School

Getting your kids through school is going to be a long, and probably difficult, part of your parental life.

If school was a bad experience in your life, you'll be visiting familiar territory when your children bring their painful school experiences home to you. If it was a good experience for you, you should be prepared to deal with the other side of the *red F*. You just may have a child who does.

There are kids who are not good at academics, just like there are kids who are not good at the arts. But we don't constantly grade (or degrade) those who can't play an instrument or draw, class after class, making them do one artistic event after another, humiliating them all the way.

But a kid who is not academically inclined is often subjected to a system that puts their shortcomings on display every day, class after class, for all their friends, classmates, and peers to see.

The world of academics quickly becomes a source of embarrassment, frustration and anger. Teachers and administrators not only misunderstand children, but often mistreat, punish, and even encourage drugging them.

I've talked to countless kids who are extremely bright, but do poorly in school. Many of these children were put on some type of "behavior" drug shortly after starting school. Not because there was anything wrong with them, but because there is something terminally wrong with our schools.

Being without a voice, most kids just swallow the bitter pill.

The labels schools put on our children, which kids are well aware of, are terribly debilitating as well. ADD (Attention Deficit Disorder), SLD (Specific Learning Disability), SED (Severely Emotionally Disabled).

How would you feel if you were given such a label?

If your child happens to be one of the many "labeled" children, it will be like a prison sentence for you as well. School systems are very good at manipulating parents. They present an understanding, tolerant and happy face at open-house or curriculum night, but a far less tolerant and accepting one for your child.

If you go against the school bureaucracy in defense of your child, you'll see the unmasked face of your school. And it's often an indifferent, self-serving, and patronizing one.

Artistic children who do not fit into the rigid academic structure, are forced to conform to a system that will likely kill any spark of artistic genius or creativity in them. Many of these children are also having their creativity muzzled by the drugs teachers and administrators often encourage.

Intelligence can be expressed in many ways which benefits society. Academic intelligence is only one form.

Imagine a world without music, laughter or the arts. A world without Brahms, Bach, Beethoven or the Beatles. Or the joy and inspiration derived from the artists and entertainers of the world. The *class-clown* may in fact be one of the most gifted among us.

Children will gravitate to what they find interesting and what they enjoy doing. I believe it's the job of our schools then to surround that child with all the tools and assistance for them to pursue these interests to their utmost ability.

When every child is encouraged to excel in their strengths, whatever they may be, with the same guidance and resources available to children who excel in academics, then we will see the genius in *every* child.

Whether it's math or music, science or sports, English or entertainment, they all contribute to the diverse society we have in America. If you chose to become a parent, it's your job to see that schools uphold this obligation to your child.

Are you equipped to handle the psychological needs, educational advocating, and career guidance for a child with academic abilities less developed than you hoped? Advocating for a "labeled" child can become as time consuming as a second job.

There's an insidious practice in our educational system of making kids feel like they're bad because they don't do well scholastically. This in turn makes them "act-up" in class. This leads to all kinds of discipline problems, parent meetings, suspensions, and many times even court appearances and fines.

Schools create so much turmoil in the life of these "labeled" kids that they often drop-out as soon as they can. Unfortunately they don't have the skills or piece of paper (diploma) needed to get a job.

Schools create the problem, but the child is punished.

When I was going to school in the 60's & 70's, students like me, although beaten, humiliated and made to feel inadequate, were still pushed through and got our diploma.

Schools no longer push kids through, they push them out, leaving the child feeling like a failure. But in fact it's the school that is failing. For every child who drops-out or is thrown-out, the school should be given a bid *red F*.

Being an entrepreneur for over twenty years, and one who was poor at academics, I meet many individuals who are survivors, not benefactors, of our school system — people who pursued their dreams, in spite of the inadequate and often abusive treatment by the academic world. And these individuals have gone on to great achievement, success and happiness.

Many people that were forced or coerced into having only academic goals, were led into unfulfilling and unhappy lives. They are now trying to get in touch with a part of themselves that was suffocated in our schools.

Schools today have become more like prisons with metal detectors, locked doors, and invasions of privacy that would be intolerable to most of us. Schools have become mini-police states that are extremely restrictive, close-minded and oppressive.

There should be a sign on the front door of most of our schools that reads: Leave your constitutional rights outside of this building. We will teach them, but not honor them.

There's been a lot written about the incidence of violence in school. We're blaming video games, music, TV, the movies..., or just about everything but the place where so much of the violence by kids is happening: schools.

Kids aren't going into movie theaters and shooting people. They're doing it in their schools. Maybe that's where the problem lies.

Schools are a primary reason for divisiveness between kids. They set up a system that alienates, labels, and segregates kids. Children who are good at academics or athletics are made to feel superior. Children who are not good at academics or athletics are made to feel inferior.

Too many parents are struggling with school bureaucracies who are using 19th century philosophy on 21st century challenges.

Too many free-thinking kids are getting silenced, non-conformist students are being punished, and academically challenged children are being humiliated.

If you have an SLD kid, he'll likely be pushed-out. An ADD child will likely be drugged-out. And an SED kid will likely drop-out.

You may have liked school or hated it, done well academically or poorly, but you've already done your time. When you have a child you're going to have to do it all over again.

Whether it was a good experience for you or not, it may be a bad one for your child. And if so, is this really a territory you want to revisit?

"Therapy, empathy, and love must replace the drugs, electro -shock, and biochemical theories of the New Psychiatry."

Peter R. Breggin, M.D., Psychiatrist, author.

Reason 21

Ritalin

We are drugging our kids at an unprecedented rate in this country. Supporting drugs for our kids is a growing trend, so you can expect a never-ending variety of drugs to make our kids "behave."

According to Gene Haislip, of the Drug Enforcement Agency, *"No other nation prescribes stimulants [Ritalin] in such volume to its children."*

In our society, it's way too easy to "fix" our children by drugging them, instead of fixing their problems. These problems usually involve the parents (or lack thereof), schools, and a society that is extremely hostile towards its children.

In America today our kids are likely to have their first drug experience in grade school. And the pushers are not shady-looking guys in back alleys, but teachers in schoolrooms. They're not pushing cocaine, they're pushing Ritalin.

Presently, Ritalin is the most widely prescribed child-control drug.

According to psychologist Linda Budd, author of Living With the Active/Alert Child, *"We've got some teachers we call 'Ritalin bullies'—he's not paying attention to me so he needs Ritalin."*

Schools once used to hit children. Now they drug them.

I was confronted with this repeatedly when my children were in grade school. Drugging my child to behave in class was compared with giving insulin to a diabetic. An absurd comparison, but one that I've heard often.

The human brain is the most complex entity in our world. What we don't know about our brain far exceeds what we do. Yet we are listening to lay people, with *no* medical experience and lots of simplistic analogies, who recommend Ritalin for our children.

High energy children, artistic children, "daydreamers," and many others that don't have their needs met by our school system often have their spirits smothered out of them with drugs they are forced to take.

These ADD children are not *suffering* from Attention Deficit Disorder, but rather they are "Alert, Decisive, Determined."

These are the future entrepreneurs, artists, musicians, and non-conformists who have historically been responsible for many of the great advancements in our civilization.

Instead of creating an environment that expands their minds, we are drugging their minds to conform to the environment.

We know for sure that all drugs have side effects. We also know that they affect children—who are still growing and developing, differently than adults. And more so than not, we find out years later that drugs we were told were harmless are in fact quite harmful.

If an Alert Decisive Determined child does get through the Ritalin mine field of school, the next big threat is the parents themselves.

You may resist the pressure from schools to drug your child, but when your child reaches adolescence, and parenting a challenging child becomes too much for you too handle, you're likely to become the next drug pusher in your child's life.

Parents, often unknowingly, spill their dysfunctions onto their children. When these dysfunctions manifest in their children's behavior, parents often choose drugging their kids. It's the easy answer.

Marriage problems, separation and divorce all have detrimental long-term effects on children. Your emotional wounds will show up in your children, even if you think you hide it from them. But drugging the kids instead of healing the adults is frequently the solution.

Therapy will often alleviate the need for these drugs. However, therapy requires parents to take some responsibility for their children's behavior and make changes in the way they handle situations.

Therapy takes time; it's not a quick fix. Drugs are a lot easier, especially since it's the child who is being forced to take them.

If you do accept the responsibility and seek help for the *family*, get ready for the next big drug pushers— insurance companies. They rarely cover family therapy adequately because it takes too much time. Insurance companies like the drugs—they're cheaper.

Children in America are being drugged, often against their will and without their consent. Kids don't have any say in the drugs that adults are shoving down their throats.

Pressure from schools, resistance to therapy by insurance companies, doctors' eagerness to prescribe them, and the fact that it doesn't require any work on the parents' part, have led to this situation.

These are not drugs to cure illness, they are drugs to control behavior.

Psychiatry has become a religion. A "chemical imbalance" diagnosis provides absolution for bad parenting and an easy way out for improperly trained teachers. But the penance is being paid by our children.

In my generation, conformity was beaten into us. Today, children who do not conform are drugged. As a recipient of the first and a witness to the second, it's difficult for me to tell which is worse.

Our children are getting the message loud and clear that drugs are the answer to their problems, and so they are trying all kinds of new and dangerous "designer" drugs.

The Ritalin they took as kids, they are now splitting open and snorting for a cocaine-like high.

According to the Drug Enforcement Agency, Ritalin is one of the top ten stolen drugs and is now being sold as a street drug.

For the foreseeable future, drugs are going to be the method of choice for controlling children. As a parent, will you be willing to resist the pressure? Even when it means changing your own actions and behavior?

As a society we need to stop the Ritalin restraints with which we're shackling our children's minds and emotions.

For updated information visit www.50reasons.com

"You will never be happy if you continue to search for what happiness consists of. You will never live if you are looking for the meaning of life."

Albert Camus (1913-60), French-Algerian philosopher.

Reason 22

To Fill A Need Within Yourself

In the classic Christmas cartoon, "Rudolph the Red Nosed Raindeer," there's a place for all the broken and neglected toys. It's called the Island of Misfit Toys.

As a child, I would feel sad watching the toys hopelessly wanting to be played with. But as a parent, I see that the misfit toys, like the children watching them, just want to be loved.

Unfortunately, many of us don't receive the love we need when we're children, and so we spend much of our lives searching for someone or something to fill the emptiness.

Like the misfit toys, we end up stranded on the Island of Unfulfilled Needs. Both are sad places.

If your parents deprived you of the love you needed, it's unlikely that anyone will be able to fill that need within you, except you.

We usually look for our needs to be filled by a lover, husband or wife, because finding the answers within ourselves is usually difficult and painful. Often we have to face issues in our life that we would rather not.

And so we bring a child into our unfulfilled life and then expect that child to provide fulfillment for us. Because our needs aren't being met by those in our life, we often unknowingly and unfairly attach this expectation to the umbilical cord of an innocent baby.

From the moment of birth, your child must take a top priority in your life.

When you become a parent to get your own needs met, your child's needs often get lost. It's difficult to provide what you're missing.

If children are used to fill the needs in their parents, the children will end up feeling empty. And they, too, will look for their needs to be satisfied in outside relationships.

Not finding the love they're seeking, they will likely follow in their parents' footsteps and make a baby—another passenger on the ship of empty souls.

By having children, we confuse our needs being filled with the reality that our life is now overflowing with the needs of others. We spend much time and energy bailing out just to stay afloat. But our needs remain floundering at the bottom, causing turbulence in our life.

If having a baby is something you're doing to bring a sense of fulfillment into your life, or if there's an emptiness inside you that you're hoping to fill, I suggest you take a "time out." Having a child to fill a need within you is likely to leave a need within your child.

A child comes into the would with lots of needs you're going to have to fill. But you can't fill another's needs if you're empty.

"No test tube can breed love and affection. No frozen packet of semen ever read a story to a sleepy child."

Shirley Williams (b. 1930), British Liberal-Democrat.

Reason 23

You Can't

Maybe the fact that you can't have children is nature's way of informing you that you shouldn't.

Destiny may have another path for you to take. Being a parent may not be the role your soul has chosen in this life. Afterall, you have already been given a life—your own.

For many, especially in the 30 to 40 age bracket, having a baby is an obsession. Many couples spend thousands of dollars trying to create life through drugs and artificial means.

This money would likely produce better results if spent on therapy, trying to find out why having a baby is so necessary for *their* lives.

No matter what the dangers of fertility drugs, or intrusiveness of some fertility treatments, having a baby becomes all consuming. Sex is replaced by science, which takes the love out of lovemaking.

We claim to be such a religious people, with a strong faith in God. Trying to have a child provides a good opportunity to put your faith to the test.

Inability to procreate is not a life-threatening condition requiring the medical sciences. Fertility drugs are not being taken to cure a disease—at least not a physical one.

Why not replace drugs from a fertility specialist,

with faith in your prayers to God? Or maybe "faith in God," although a good slogan, isn't reliable enough for you.

It appears that many aren't willing to accept the outcome. In 1997, there was a big event publicized throughout the country. A church going, God-fearing couple from Iowa who met through bible school had seven children as a result of taking fertility drugs.

Obviously faith and trusting in God wasn't reliable enough for them. They referred to it as *Seven from Heaven*, but in reality it was a *multitude from Metrodin* (a fertility drug).

Humans aren't supposed to have litters. God or nature didn't design us for that. Dogs have litters, but a female dog also has ten breasts; the last I noticed, women still have only two.

There are consequences of using fertility drugs. According to Dr. Carl Weiner, director of the Center for Advanced Fetal Care at the University of Maryland School of Medicine, *"Mothers of multiples have higher rates of depression and divorce."*

What gets little publicity is that these infants were born prematurely and not fully developed. Such infants often have difficulty breathing and are likely to have cardiovascular problems, bowel disorders, and a host of other medical problems throughout their life.

Along with potential health risks, families often have more children than they can care for.

The *Metrodin* family from Iowa is going to, "totally rely on the fact that God is going to raise these kids."

They didn't rely on God to have them, but now expect God to care for them.

We have reached a point in our evolution where we can create human life in a test tube. Soon we may be able to create human life through cloning. But just because we *can* doesn't mean we *should*.

Breeding a baby in a test tube, or in another person's body, is using science without ethics.

There is a place for science in childbirth. But common sense, reason, and ethics are blurred when a person is blinded by a single want, and a profession blinded by the almighty dollar.

Some of the artificial methods being used today are going to have lifelong consequences for children conceived in this way.

Just think how depressing it's going to be for the child who grows up, traces his routes, and finds that it leads to a sperm bank.

"Children begin by loving their parents. After a time they judge them. Rarely, if ever, do they forgive them."

Oscar Wilde (1854-1900), Playwright, author.

Reason 24

You Will Be Held Accountable

Parents are held accountable for their actions far more today than in past generations. Holding one's parents accountable is a necessary step in breaking patterns of subtle and obvious abuse.

Today's kids are already a step ahead in asking tough questions about our past, and questioning our present. Like it or not, this is a trend destined to continue.

As a parent, no matter how good your intentions may be or how hard you try, you're going to make lots of mistakes. You probably won't recognize most of them—but your children will.

Sooner or later the blinders of mistaken loyalty get removed, and at some point your child is going to look at the decisions you made through the eyes of an adult.

It wasn't until I was forty that I was able to look back at some of the things done to me by my parents, and things that weren't done which should have been.

My parents would often tell me they were going to beat the "living daylights" out of me.

As a child, I thought the bright flashes of light I would see while being shaken by my mother or beaten by my father were my "living daylights." I thought they were something bad, and all I wanted was for them to go out.

I now understand that those bright lights were being caused by my brain slamming against my skull. And I wonder how close my parents came to putting out my *living* daylights.

The abuse and mistreatment being done to today's children is different than when I was a child. Hopefully fewer parents are beating the "living daylights" out of their kids, although too many still do. But emotional neglect and abuse, which may be more subtle, are just as prevalent today and just as damaging.

Parents tend to brush off the bad, as if it should be outweighed by the good they do. But a weekend outing doesn't replace a week of coming home late. Buying your daughter new shoes doesn't cushion the impact of not attending her dance recital. An ice cream cone after a slap across the face doesn't melt the sting—physically or emotionally.

Some day these children will become adults, who will again ask—Why? Why didn't you go to marriage counseling before walking out? Why did you drug *me* with Ritalin, when you were so screwed up? Why didn't you accept the person I was? Why didn't you tell me you loved me? Why didn't you show me that you loved me? Why did you have me??

Just when you think your children are out of your thinning hair, they're going to want to drag you—probably kicking and screaming—into therapy. And then you're going to hear just how terrible you were as their parent.

After all the trials and tribulation of being a parent, you'll likely be faced with the fact that your children hold you accountable for many of the bad things in their lives.

This may be one of the most difficult challenges of being a parent, because it will likely happen long after your children have grown up and left home. And there is a good chance you will be totally unaware of your child's feelings.

Good parenting requires holding your children accountable when they are young. Good parenting also requires *you* to accept accountability when they're grown.

Their minds will want answers, because their emotions need healing, for their hearts to find happiness.

You can accept their grievances without ex-cuses—and show that you still love your child, or smother yourself in denial and anger—and lose your child.

When it comes to parenting, kids give the grades. You may not like the mark you'll get, but as parents often tell their children: "You get the mark you deserve."

"When angry, count ten, before you speak; if very angry, a hundred."

Thomas Jefferson (1743-1826), U.S. president.

Reason 25

You're A Hollerer Or A Screamer

One of my many parenting flaws has been that I holler. I used to rationalize that hollering wasn't as bad as hitting, so therefore it was OK. This incorrect rationale made it easy to ignore my own shortcomings as a parent.

Hollering or screaming usually starts when our children are just babies. They're effective because a loud voice is scary. And they become an easy way to handle difficult situations.

But it's really a form of bullying and intimidation. It requires no parenting skills; in fact it usually indicates a lack of these skills.

When you have kids, there are times when your hollering or screaming will be almost impossible to control. The problem occurs when yelling becomes a chosen method of parenting.

Screaming sets parents on a dangerous course of scaring children into desired behaviors, and making their kids fear them. As the child gets older, the fear will have to become more terrifying. If the behavior gets worse, the fear factor can become dangerous.

When we lose control of our emotions and resort to being loud, all kinds of negative energy within us is triggered. It clouds our thinking, poisons our tongue, and makes it easy to say things that are mean and hurtful.

As parents, we often forget what we say. However, the words we scream at our children often have a negative and long term effect.

When I holler at my kids, I often say the same hateful words that were said to me by my parents, even though these words are not a part of my vocabulary. Hearing them as a child was horrible, and yet I repeat them.

Hollering seems to shut off all the higher parts of my brain and healthier parts of my emotions.

All children react to hollering differently. For some it builds defiance, for others it breaks their spirit. I've found that it usually leaves them feeling angry and hurt instead of sorry for what they did. Screaming usually drowns out the message.

Hollering or screaming causes adrenaline to be pumped through our body. Anger and adrenaline are a scary combination. They make it easy to cross over the line and get physical. All it takes is for one wrong button to be pushed. Children, especially adolescents, will inevitably push it.

If you were raised in a family where there was hollering and screaming, you will likely do the same. As parents we tend to stick with what we know—which is usually what our parents did.

I'm sure some research scientist is going to try and blame hollering on genetics as well. But the simple truth is: the flaws in a parent's character often become part of a child's personality.

Hollering and screaming are like blunt objects, pounding on the emotions of a child. But the words are usually razor shape. The wounds they cause, which are invisible to most of us, will likely go untreated and leave scars for life.

If you're going to have a child, give your kid a break. Break the hollering and screaming habit.

To add your opinion go to www.50reasons.com

"Children seldom have a proper sense of their own tragedy, discounting and keeping hidden the true horrors of their short lives..."

Shirley Hazzard (b. 1931), Author

Reason 26

You Believe in Corporal Punishment (Hitting)

Hitting hurts emotions. Hitting teaches hitting. Hitting promotes violence. Hitting doesn't work. Hitting is wrong! All that being said, I hate to admit that I've done it.

When my sons were in diapers I would give them an occasional whack on their diapered butt. I didn't think spanking was really hitting. To me, hitting was across the face.

I thought the whack on the butt was OK because they couldn't understand language yet. But it was I who didn't understand language—a baby's language.

During the diaper years, my sons got along pretty well. But they were almost always under their mother's or my watchful eyes.

If one hit the other, my wife or I would usually spank the one who did the hitting. Since people would often comment on how well behaved they were, the authoritarian approach seemed to be working pretty well.

Once they grew out of the diaper phase, I stopped hitting them. Their mother would still smack them on the hand, but I would rarely say anything. I thought it was important that I support her.

I would often threaten to hit, but I never wanted to cross over that line. I took great pride in the fact that I wasn't hitting my kids.

Then came adolescence. The method my sons chose to resolve issues between themselves was hitting. As teenagers, the hitting became fist fights.

One night I was awakened to the rumble of bodies being thrown against walls, banging into furniture, as the hitting turned to punching.

I warned them repeatedly that I was going to "give them a taste of their own medicine." On that night I would cross that line, but the bitter medicine was mine to taste.

There is a different kind of pain that comes from being hit by a parent. It is not like a fight at school or a teacher hitting you, which was very common not so long ago.

I know first hand how much damage hitting does to the emotions of a child. Being slapped across the face by my father throughout my childhood has left permanent scars on me. My face would get red, but that faded. My emotions bled, and that went undetected.

I separated my sons, slapped them both across the face, repeatedly, and then went to my bedroom and cried my eyes out.

All the pain I felt as a child, being slapped across the face, was stinging more than when it actually happened. Because I now new I had inflicted that same pain on my children.

I suffered from depression for years until I confronted my father with what his hitting did to me. I know that the pain from being hit lingers long after the sting wears off. And I feared that my hitting my own sons would escalate, as it did with my father.

I didn't sleep that night. I spent the night looking through the phone book for therapists, and the next day on the phone talking with counselors.

With family therapy and by attending parenting classes, I slowly began seeing how my behavior, past and present, had molded my children into who they were.

I didn't want to see this, but I had to face it for my children's sake. I love my sons with all my heart and soul, but I didn't like who they were. And who they were, **was me**.

I read the research on hitting and how it affects everything from self-esteem, to eating disorders, to a child's IQ, not to mention all the studies that relate hitting to violence.

In my experience, hitting *appeared* to have some short-term benefits, but it wreaked long-term havoc in my family.

I watch therapist after therapist on television warning new and would-be parents against hitting and offering alternatives to hitting. Hearing therapists describe the negative consequences of hitting, I have living proof that they are right.

It's difficult for some people to admit that a method of parenting used for so long can be so wrong.

In 1978, Sweden enacted laws prohibiting corporal punishment. At that time 70% of the population was opposed to such laws. But after virtually eradicating this destructive behavior, the Swedes have had a chance to see the positive results.

Twenty years later, only 10% remain opposed: a remarkable popularity that few, if any, initiatives ever achieve.

In America we are moving away from hitting children as well. Hitting is fast and easy, but it is a primitive and unenlightened response.

Altering behavior through non-violent methods is challenging. Modeling calm, confident behavior as a parent requires emotional strength.

If we truly want to stop violence, we first have to stop it in the home.

Years of counseling has helped my family get through this painful time. Counseling has also shown me alternatives that work better than hitting and have long-term benefits.

But these methods have as much to do with how I react as they do with what my children may have done. I am held accountable as well.

When we started family therapy I thought modeling was a child's hobby. I've found out it's a parent's job — role modeling.

And one final thought: As adults, if someone assaults us on the street or in our home, we have the law on our side. If someone were to hit us, or even verbally assault us at work, we have the law to defend us. If our children were to hit **us**, we would again have the law on our side.

Isn't it only fair that the laws which protect adults also protect those most incapable of protecting themselves—children?

When parents stop hitting their children, our society will begin healing, one family at a time.

The benefits of not hitting will be far reaching. Your children will benefit, your grandchildren will benefit, and you will benefit, in knowing that you took one more step up the ladder of enlightened parenting.

"Animals are such agreeable friends - they ask no questions, they pass no criticisms."

George Eliot (1819-80), English novelist.

Reason 27

You Won't Share Your Home With A Dog

Having a child requires many sacrifices. Because owning a dog brings additional work for a family, it may be rejected easily. But what a dog brings to a child's life is extremely beneficial.

If you are not willing to make this sacrifice for your child, you need to consider what sacrifices you will make.

All families have their share of emotional wounds. But I truly believe that a dog can do more good for the emotional health of a family than any pill from a psychiatrist's storehouse of drugs.

What a dog brings to a child's life is immeasurable; what it brings to a family is priceless.

I didn't have a dog when I was a child. But like all kids, I really wanted one. My mother did not want one because it would have "dirtied" her house. My father did not want one because, well, he didn't like any "inconveniences" in his life.

When my two boys were 4 and 5 years old, I decided that they were going to have the companionship of a dog. I thought it would teach them responsibility by giving them the responsibility of caring for another life. And I believed it would nurture within them a kindness towards animals.

I wasn't sure whether I wanted our dog to live in our home or outside in a dog house. But a good friend and animal lover reminded me that dogs are pack animals, they need to either be with other dogs or people, but not alone.

This made sense to me. Our dog was going to be a member of our family, instead of a lawn ornament. I purchased a black Labrador retriever and named him Zack.

Over the years, Zack became not just a part of our family, but the favorite in our family. At one time or another we all couldn't stand being around each other, but no one ever minded being around Zack. In fact it was those times when everyone wanted Zack to be with them.

There were times when my children's world was being shattered by the adult one in which they were born. It was with our dog they often found comfort.

They snuggled up with Zack on the floor, reas-suring *him* that everything was going to be all right.

From hearing them talk to Zack, I learned how important it is for a child to be heard — even if it's only by a dog.

There will be many times when you are so busy with life's obligations that you will not have time to listen to your child. It will be the dog to whom your child will turn.

Dogs can be like guardian angels for children.

When one of us hollered at Zack to "get out of the way" because we were being impatient, he would scurry out of the way with his head down and tail between his legs, afraid that he did something wrong.

Ultimately whoever yelled at him inevitably felt bad, petted him, and said they were sorry.

Lessons are learned by little things like these.

It did not matter to our dog that he didn't deserve to be hollered at. He forgave us and wagged his tail with delight when we would pet him.

In a family, forgiveness is as necessary as wind to a sail. We all hurt one another at various times. It is forgiveness that allows a family to move forward. A dog demonstrates instant and unconditional forgiveness.

A dog can help reduce stress in parents, as well. When I was miserable and no one wanted to be near me, when even I didn't want to be near me, my dog would snuggle his head against my arm. As I laid my hand on his head, I could feel the tension drain from my body.

Dogs are like emotional sponges. They absorb bad emotions, and give back undying loyalty, affection and love.

In our "dump them in daycare" society, a dog is a dependable source of security. Coming home from school, the latch-key kid will open the door to the wagging tail of a faithful friend, instead of the stillness of an empty house.

The joy that a dog brings to a child's life is boundless. A dog is a boy's best buddy and a girl's greatest gift.

For the happiness a dog will bring into your child's life, are you willing to share your home with a dog?

Postscript:

During the writing of this book our dog, Zack, passed away. He was old and it was peaceful, but it was a devastating loss. Yet even in this heartbreaking experience my children have learned one of life's most difficult lessons—how to deal with death. My sons have now had a chance to reflect on having Zack in their lives, and this is what they had to say:

Joseph: "The best thing about my dog was that he was always there for me, to listen to me, or play with me, or do anything. And he was always happy as can be just to be doing things with me. It never mattered what, just as long as he was with me, he was happy. And he wasn't afraid of the dark when I was."

Justin: "I was 4 years old and a little scared when we got Zack, but I got really attached to him. Dogs always listen and never judge. We always felt safe with Zack in the house. And whenever I got sick, he would always lay right by me. On the last night he was with us he was real sick and came in my room so I could take care of him, and I laid right by him. He was one of the best things that ever happened to me. I still miss him, but I'm so glad we had Zack in our family."

For more heartwarming dog stories visit www.50reasons.com

"How easy for those who do not bulge
To not overindulge!"

Ogden Nash (1902-1971), U.S. poet.

Reason 28

You'll Get Fat

For good or bad, most red-blooded Americans spend the majority of their lives trying not to become fat. Nothing throws a bigger monkey-wrench into this already difficult quest than having a baby.

And this does not just pertain to women. Many men get big bellies during their wife's pregnancy.

The fact that a pregnant woman is eating for two, and that pregnancy gives a green light to eating all kinds of foods, makes it easy for caloric intake to go way up. And it is not too long before you are *both* eating for two, then three. . .

When my wife was pregnant with our first son, she developed a habit of waking up in the middle of the night to eat cookies and milk.

Before the pregnancy, I never got up in the middle of the night for anything. Well, occasionally middle-of-the-night sex would get me up, but that was pretty rare.

By the 3rd month, I was getting up and having cookies with her every night. By the 5th month it was an anticipated affair. "Good night" was replaced with "See you for cookies."

By the 7th month, we were getting up separately to have our cookies. We would mumble at each other as we crossed paths, as we went about *our* little ritual.

The novelty was gone and the only thing left was the weight we put on.

By the 9th month we both had stretched the scale springs. Overnight (a long night) my wife was 8 pounds, 7 ounces lighter, but I was still 10 pounds heavier. So much for this being only a women thing.

When we started our evening cookie raids, neither one of us realized that it would turn into a lifelong "battle of the bulge."

And so in tribute to our quoted poet, here is a little poem of my own:

From the time of your first child,

it becomes quite apparent.

Putting on weight goes hand in hand,

with being a parent.

For diet information visit www.50reasons.com

"All animals, except man, know that the principal business of life is to enjoy it."

Samuel Butler (1835-1902), Author.

Reason 29

You Can Have A Lot More Fun

My child-free friends stay as long as they are enjoying themselves at the office party. I have to leave just when the fun begins. They go to fine restaurants for romantic evenings. I go to McDonalds for *Happy Meals*. They go home and make love on the living room floor. I go home and clean the toys off the play room floor.

Having children must compensate for the fun things we give up, right? I'm not so sure.

It's hard to look at families logically, without all the emotion. But when you do, you find that most of your time is spent away from your children, upholding your parental obligations.

The time spent with your children likely involves doing homework, correcting them for doing something you do not approve of, or making them do their chores.

Two of the biggest obstacles to having fun in this life are not enough money, and not enough time. Having a child taxes your income more than Uncle Sam; and time goes by faster than a 15-minute massage.

Life becomes an accelerating tread-mill. You expend most of your energy keeping up with the demands of being a parent, which is an endless string of responsibilities, obligations and needs to be met—all except yours.

If you end up in one of the fastest growing minorities - single parents, FUN takes on a new meaning: **F**rustrated **U**naccepted **N**eglected.

Meeting someone and having a social life is more labor than fun. Not that dating as an adult is fun without kids, but with kids it becomes nightmarish.

If you are fortunate enough to have the opportunity to take a vacation, the choice will be for entertaining your children, not enlightening yourself.

It is more likely you will be standing in line at Hershey Park than reading hieroglyphics at an Egyptian pyramid.

With children, planning and packing before a vacation usually takes longer than the vacation lasts. After a vacation, it's unpacking, enough laundry for a month, and credit card bills for a year.

Are we having fun yet?

During the middle school years I was chauffeuring my kids, while my child-free friends were sunning on their decks. I bought an aluminum pool for my kids to play in, they bought a whirlpool for themselves to play in.

I attend school concerts, they attend rock concerts. OK, it's the geriatric rock crowd, but they have the time and money to go—with no baby-sitter worries. Yearly pilgrimages to the New Orleans Jazz Festival for them, monthly pilgrimages to the orthodontist for me.

And during all these years that my child-free friends were spending money enjoying themselves, they still were able to save for a summer cottage, or a nice retirement fund.

My savings, when there is any, goes for college. And as for my retirement, well.., I just hope there's still a social security fund.

It is not that you don't have fun with your children, it's just that when you spread it out over 18 or so years, it's really out of balance. The financial, physical and emotional responsibility that is required to raise healthy children takes most of the fun out of it.

Coach a baseball team. You can have a lot of fun with lots of kids, and they will remember you forever. Or better yet, spend a few days with a friend who has kids, and see who is having more fun.

"Prejudice. A vagrant opinion without visible means of support."

Ambrose Bierce (1842-1914), Author.

Reason 30

You're Prejudiced

If I had a dollar for every racist who claimed they weren't prejudice, I'd be in a financial bracket with Bill Gates. Just because you don't wear a sheet, burn crosses or secretly admire Hitler, doesn't mean you're not prejudice.

I know a lot of nice people who harbor nasty prejudices.

When I was growing up the N-word was used regularly in my home. When Martin Luther King was assassinated my father celebrated. And **no one** in my family believed they were prejudice.

There are millions of families just like my childhood family. I call them *church-going bigots.* They claim they are not prejudice while regularly spilling hatred and intolerance onto their innocent children.

Like second-hand smoke—the toxin is coming out of the parents and poisoning the children.

In America, more than in any other country, prejudice is contrary to everything that makes us great as a nation.

We are the most powerful, most technologically advanced, most athletic, most artistic and most dynamic country in the world. America continues to prove the *melting-pot* is the way to greatness.

To instill resistance to diversity in your children is to set them sailing into life heading in the wrong direction with an old, worn out, tattered sail, and expecting them to navigate. The sea of acceptance will swallow your prejudiced offspring.

Prejudice eats away at the soul of a family like cancer. Happiness can not grow in soil of hate—no matter how subtle the hatred or how it's disguised.

The prejudice harboring in your heart, no matter how subtle, will be passed on to your children. It is what's in your heart that nourishes your children. Why leave a rotten seed that could potentially poison them?

You have an obligation to explore the true depth of prejudice within yourself and your mate before you bring another life into this ever-melding world.

"I am afraid we must make the world honest before we can honestly say to our children that honesty is the best policy."

George Bernard Shaw (1856-1950), Playwright.

Reason 31

You Believe Honesty Is *Always* The Best Policy

Like many other virtues, honesty is relative. Many extenuating circumstances influence how it will be applied, and to what degree—the very nature of which is in some degree dishonest.

In many cases, lying may be the best policy. This is true for issues that range from: "Of course there is a Santa Clause," to "We didn't have sex until we were married."

Having developed as a child in the fertile soil of the 1960's and sprouted in the freedom of the 1970's, I was determined to be open and honest with my children. But what seemed right at 20 didn't seem so right at 35.

I started out as a parent thinking honesty was always the best policy. But the price for my honesty was paid by my children, as they began acting-out what they knew their father did.

"You did this when you were a kid and you turned out OK," became a constant reminder that honesty is *not* always the best policy.

I've since learned to selectively choose when to be honest, to what degree to be honest, and equally important, when to lie. Not all lies are bad.

I know this flies in the face of what is happening in society today. But reality isn't always what society wishes it was.

If we were really honest, we would acknowledge that everybody lies at some time in their life. In fact, most of us continue to lie throughout our lives. Whether it's a lie by omission, or a so-called "white lie," a lie is a lie!

Did you ever drink and drive? Did you ever get into a car when the driver was drinking? The honest answer to both is yes. So did almost everybody else I knew—adults included.

In the early 1970's, this was pretty much considered acceptable behavior. Drinking and driving in the "Frank Sinatra Generation" was even more flagrant.

Do I want my kids to know this? Absolutely not! I have seen how my behavior (past and present) influences my children's actions. My kids and their friends enjoy stories about the 70's and often ask all the wrong questions.

I now skirt the truth, lie by omission, and even recall bad things that never really happened, because I know it is a different world in which my children live in. The rules, laws, and expectations of society are different today.

By choosing honesty, I would likely leave them with a false and potentially deadly sense of approval.

As a parent, the highest responsibility is to the healthy development of your child, not to a principle—noble as it may be. You should not give a child a knife until he is capable of handling it. The same can be argued for honesty.

Lying is also a part of being a child—it is as natural as wetting the bed occasionally. All too often the lie creates an out of focus view of the incident, and quickly dominates the event.

More can be learned in trying to get behind the reason for the lie, than just coming down hard on a child for fibbing.

Still not convinced? Take a look at the consequences in a world where honesty reigns supreme:

➢ Never having a surprise party.

➢ Terminating all covert military affairs and undercover police work.

➢ Never asking: Do you like my new hair style? Do I look fat? Was it good for you?

➢ Having our spouses know everything we did before we met. And eventually, how much we miss it.

➢ Never being able to spare another's feelings. A terrible cook. A terminally ill child. No exceptions!

➢ Having to come to a COMPLETE stop at EVERY stop sign. Or voluntarily fessing-up!

➢ Ending the myth of Santa Clause, the Tooth Fairy, the Easter Bunny and all other childhood wonders.

It is a mistaken belief that if something is right, it's always right—no exceptions! Human nature tends not to support absolutes in any form.

There is sometimes a duty higher than honesty. And being a parent is one.

"The advantages of extended breast-feeding are indeed indisputable and include nutritional, immunological, and psychological benefits to both infant and mother, as well as economic benefits."

American Dietetic Association

Reason 32

You Won't Breast Feed Your Child

Being born in the 1950's I was part of the first generation of children to be raised on man-made formula instead of mother's milk. I am also a part of the most breast-obsessed generation of men ever to walk upright on this planet.

Whether there's a link between the two is anybody's guess.

However, there are some things we don't have to guess about when it comes to breast feeding. It is universally accepted today that the advice doctors were giving in the 1950's and 60's was wrong: Formula is not better than mother's milk.

For mom, breast feeding is one of the most nurturing and bonding experiences in life. For dad, well, when you hear that crying in the middle of the night because the baby's hungry, it needs its mommy. Dad can sleep like a baby.

And so, in the spirit of David Letterman, the *Top Ten* reasons to breast feed your baby are:

Top Ten Reasons to Breast Feed Your Baby

10: Breastfed children have higher IQ's.

9: You will save $1000 a year in formula, bottles, etc.

8: The American Academy of Pediatrics says so.

7: Your child will have fewer ear infections.

6: Breastfed children have fewer allergies.

5: Michael Jordan was breastfed.

4: Breastfed children are thinner - throughout life.

3: You will lose weight faster.

2: It reduces your risk of breast cancer.

And the Number One reason to breast feed your baby!

1: God (or nature) wasn't wrong.

For more information on breastfeeding visit www.50reasons.com

"It is change, continuing change, inevitable change, that is the dominant factor in society today. No sensible decision can be made any longer without taking into account not only the world as it is, but the world as it will be.."

Isaac Asimov (1920-1992), Author

Reason 33

You're Resistant to Change

Our world is changing faster than a Pentium processor could keep up with. The ability to change will be as necessary for the survival of children in the Twenty-First Century as farming the land was to the children of the Nineteenth Century.

One of the things that makes America great is our ability to change, and change rapidly when necessary. As a nation we may be one big dysfunctional family, but our ability to change helps keep us together.

There are many among us who fight change with every bit of bull-headed denial we have. Change ruffles our Ostrich feathers, and we would rather keep our heads buried in the past.

However, progress is coming on all fronts. Change is not just going to continue, but expand. Not embracing change will cause disharmony in your life, and could cause disaster in your child's life.

In today's world, things change almost daily. The laws, expectations, and rules of society change just as fast. Keeping abreast of technology and the expanding economy, your child must be able to accept change and take advantage of it.

The way you handle change in your life, big and small, will be the example you set for your children.

Change is a scary thing for most of us, and that is quite normal. But change is an area in which we must confront our fears, whether our fears emanate from new technology or new ideas.

Like a roller-coaster, it's only scary hearing the clicking up the first hill. After that, the forces of nature take over. It may be terrifying. It may be fun. It may make you laugh or make you scream, but at the end of the ride, you'll have a smile on your face. Change can be exhilarating.

Along with the willingness to accept change must be the strength to change things that have become harmful habits or addictions in your life, or behaviors that you know will be unhealthy for your child. Changes that you must make first, so as not to infect an innocent new life.

Join the enlightened age and embrace change in your life. Then, if you bring children into the world, you can embrace them with the wisdom of the 21st century.

"A custom loathsome to the eye, hateful to the nose, harmful to the brain, dangerous to the lungs, and in the black, stinking fume thereof nearest resembling the horrible Stygian smoke of the pit that is bottomless."

James I of England (1566-1625).

Reason 34

You Smoke

Obviously the dangers of smoking have been known for quite some time. Old James I of England new it in the 1500's. In the 21st century, cigarette smoking will be viewed much like the black-plague was in James I's time.

If you are a smoker, you've already been lectured to, preached at, and ostracized by society. This book is not going to do any of that, even though I'm an ex-smoker—and you know all that goes along with that!

Yes, I hate cigarettes and I hate cigarette smoke, but I don't hate smokers. Because I still love my sons.

Both my children got sucked into smoking. And *you* know the hell that it's going to be for them to quit.

My younger son has tried quitting many times and hopefully this time he'll make it.

My older son is terribly addicted. He tried quitting once or twice, but it was so hard that he won't even try anymore. Since he was 19 years old, he's been hacking up disgusting black stuff in the morning.

No matter how you feel about smoking today, you will not want your child to go through this addiction tomorrow.

Society has finally put a muzzle on the biggest drug pushers in America—giant tobacco companies, by taking down the glamorous billboards tobacco companies have strung up across America. It's going to be a little harder for them to poison the kids of the future with advertising.

You will be the billboard for your children. Your children will look up to you like they look up to no one else. Society is trying to remove cigarettes from your child's world, but only you can remove them from your child's life.

"Drunkenness is nothing but voluntary madness"
Seneca (c.5B.C.- A.D.65), Roman writer, philosopher.

Reason 35

More Than One Person Has Said You Have
a Drinking Problem

Maybe it is voluntary. Maybe it is genetic. Maybe it is a learned habit. Everybody has their own opinion. But, if more than one person - family or friend, says you have a drinking problem—you have a drinking problem, at least as it pertains to being a parent.

More children's lives are ruined by alcoholism than by any other addiction—legal or illegal. When you hear screwed-up adults talking about their early life, their stories almost always involve one, or both, parents abusing alcohol.

Drinking is your addiction, but it will poison your children just as sure as it is poisoning your liver.

For most alcoholics, it is not until they hit bottom that they acknowledge drinking is a problem. But as you spiral to hell, you are bringing your innocent child with you.

The damage your addiction causes will likely last throughout your child's life. It is one of life's most unfair consequences—a parent abuses alcohol and the children suffer a lifetime hangover.

Alcoholics rarely see the damage they cause. Unfortunately, alcoholics rarely listen to reason either. So rather than repeat what you've already heard, probably dozens of times, perhaps you will consider the following: All kids are going to do for you is cut into your drinking time and cost you a lot of money that could be spent at the bar.

Before long they are going to be stealing your booze and probably sharing it with their friends. And you will likely have to go pick them up at either the police station or the hospital.

Getting up with a hangover to the sound of a crying baby, school problems, auto accidents, etc., etc., etc. You get the picture.

And after all is said and done, your kids will grow up to either hate you for your drinking, or be just like you. It's a lose/lose situation.

If you can't stop drinking for the sake of your children, then don't have children for the sake of your drinking.

"No matter how calmly you try to referee, parenting will eventually produce bizarre behavior, and I'm not talking about the kids. Their behavior is always normal."

Bill Cosby (b. 1937), Comedian, actor, author.

Reason 36

You're Not Qualified

Throughout our history the only qualifications for having children were: A spouse, hatchable eggs, and sperm that could swim. If a couple met those qualifications they were pretty much considered qualified.

Today, even that is too many qualifications. You don't really need a spouse any more. You can buy sperm. You can also buy an egg. You can even rent a body to inject and carry it all.

A person can lack the skills to take care of his or her own life, but can still create a new life. No instruction, training, or experience is necessary before having children. There are people all around having kids who aren't qualified to have a pet.

The only child raising experience most people get is from our parents, who were doing what their parents did. Basically we are using the parenting infrastructure of the 20th century, trying to navigate our children through the 21st century.

Using outdated parenting methods undermines our society. It is time to re-tool parenting in America.

As I started experiencing challenges with my sons, I quickly discovered that my lack of experience left me with few choices in dealing with these new situations. It didn't take long before my storehouse of mostly useless and often harmful parenting skills was empty.

Even though making a child comes naturally, parenting a child does not. Just like in a job or business, there are lots of little tricks that can make parenting easier.

Parenting classes are available just like computer classes. However, few people acknowledge they need help.

Not only can we learn successful parenting methods, we can learn to see the things we do as parents that actually cause some of the problems in our children.

Parenting classes clearly need to be expanded, and publicized more. A good place to start would be to add a fourth R to our educational agenda: Reading, wRiting, aRithmetic and Raising children.

Our schools teach a lot of things that have about as much application in the real world as a Mother Goose fairy tale.

Most children will grow up and have their own children. They may not need to know where Zimbabwe is, or its chief export, but they will need to know something about caring for children and the challenges that will be experienced. They will need to know not just the biology but the practicality, even if it just helps them become better baby-sitters.

Before having children of your own, work with kids in some capacity by volunteering at a children's hospital, or at a school lunch room. Be an aide in a daycare center. Forget about the money — you're doing it for the experience it will give you today, and the benefits it will provide your child tomorrow.

But at the very least, accept the fact that having a baby does not make you qualified to raise a child.

Things you can do to gain experience:

➢ Taking parenting classes.

➢ Reading books on parenting.

➢ Becoming a Teacher's Aide.

➢ Baby-sitting for neighbors, family or friends.

➢ Getting involved in community events for children, or better yet - starting one.

➢ Talking to children.

➢ Working with juvenile delinquents.

➢ Tutoring.

➢ Mentoring.

➢ Hosting a child from another country.

➢ And most important - *listening* to children.

"It is easier to live through someone else than to become complete yourself."

Betty Friedan (b.1921), Writer

Reason 37

You're Lonely

For many people, children have become the remedy of choice to cure loneliness.

Many of us don't really trust that the opposite sex can or will provide a lifetime of companionship, loyalty and love. So a child appears to be the miracle prescription to rid our life of loneliness.

Whenever we use children in an attempt to heal our emotions or fill a need within ourselves, that yellow flag of caution should start waving in front of us. Because on some level, we are creating a life to provide a cure, and putting the needs of the child behind us.

Loneliness comes from something missing within us, not around us. A child, a spouse, or even stardom can not cure loneliness.

Marylyn Monroe was surrounded by people, adored by millions, and loved by every man who saw her; and yet she died a very lonely woman.

There are many people with children who are very lonely.

Being alone is a situation; being lonely is some-thing deeper. There are reasons why we *feel* lonely.

A baby will change the situation, but the underly-ing emotion will remain. A baby is not qualified, nor should be expected to fill an emotional void in you, that was probably left in you by someone else.

A child may initially make the feeling of loneliness disappear from your life. But I think we all know that disappearing is just magic. It's still there somewhere. And when you look behind the curtain, you'll probably find your child has it.

The way happy people spread happiness, and optimistic people spread optimism, lonely people spread loneliness.

Why are you lonely? Find the honest answer to that question, even if it means getting some counseling, and you can rid your life of loneliness. And isn't that what you really want?

"Distrust everyone in whom the impulse to punish is powerful!"

Friedrich Nietzsche (1844-1900), German philosopher.

Reason 38

We're Outlawing Everything Kids Do

In one form or another we are outlawing being a kid. Kids are under attack on all fronts. There are more laws aimed at kids (under 18) than ever before, and for some reason we've decided that we're going to enforce these laws on this generation of kids more aggressively than ever before.

What kids like doing, adults have historically liked preventing. Only today, we're making what kids like doing illegal.

Standing around on a corner, or "hanging-out," will get a kid harassed by the police and possibly a citation. If any parks are close by, they're usually closed at night—at least to kids. Even when the parks are open, the activities kids want to do are often forbidden.

Towns across America have outlawed activities such as skateboarding, roller blading, and many X Games and sports that are so popular with this generation.

Hanging out on a corner or in a park is what most teenagers enjoy doing. It's a healthy part of growing up. But a group of kids, being kids, has become a bad thing—regardless of what they are doing.

In a large part because of media hype, many adults are fearful of a group of kids, for no other reason than they look different—maybe even bizarre. And because they have a lot of youthful exuberance they are often physical and make noise.

My son and a group of fourteen year old boys were hanging around outside an ice cream & pizza shop at 7:30 PM on a Friday night, and ended up with citations. The citation stated: *"Actor engaged in tumultuous behavior making unreasonable noise thereby creating offensive condition serving no legitimate purpose."*

What?? I thought that having fun was a legitimate purpose for kids.

The ice cream & pizza shop didn't complain. There were no fights, no guns and no vandalism. But there was noise and rough play.

Many of us would like children to be seen and not heard. But, apparently, even being seen is too much for some.

Another way our society outlaws what kids do is with our "anti-kid" zoning laws. And how easily local politicians capitulate when confronted by the same tired voices every time a youth-oriented facility is proposed. The urban-sprawl we have allowed is squeezing out our children.

The few places that remain for our youth to hang out are often closed or restricted. Of course it's always vandalism that's used as a reason to ban kids.

Maybe it's time we start looking at the vandalism adults are doing to our children's world.

We paved over the fields our children should be running through. We polluted the waters our children should be swimming in. And we built shopping centers on the playgrounds our children should be playing in.

When an entrepreneur in a neighboring town wanted to buy an old food store and turn it into a place for skateboarding, with video games and a host of other entertainment for teenagers, the town was in an uproar. It was stopped.

When a movie theater complex was proposed in my town with attractions for kids, the vocal minority was contentious. Instead we got another shopping center.

When our high school wanted to put up lights on the football field so kids could have safe and supervised events at night, that vocal minority again spilled its anti-kid venom and killed the lights.

Take a look at your town. How many establishments cater to the needs of adults? Bars, restaurants, malls, shopping centers, etc. Now, how many places cater to the needs of kids? And how many of them are available when the kids want to use them?

Adults have created a 24-hour society so we can have our needs met anytime we choose. But our kids are being squeezed out.

There is even a town in New Jersey that has outlawed the ice-cream truck from playing the ice-cream song, "because several residents complained to officials that the repetitious music was a nuisance."

We have other subtle ways of outlawing what kids do. The current trend to make all kids dress alike in schools is just another form of outlawing individual expression. And if a kid challenges the rules, the parents will eventually end up in trouble with the law.

Striping away what little civil rights our children have is how we are responding to violence in schools. This is because it is much easier than dealing with the real issues.

Get tough with kids! That's the cry ringing out across America. Mandatory sentences! Try them as adults! Send them to adult prisons!

The more caged-in and restricted our kids feel, the more they are going to lash out. The more adults lash out with vengeance, the more kids will seek vengeance. The more our youths feel violated by the law, the more they will violate it.

We can't teach individual liberty in school class-rooms and deny it in school handbooks. We can't continue to outlaw being a kid and expect our kids not to be outlaws.

"If there is a species which is more maltreated than children, then it must be their toys..."

Jean Baudrillard (b. 1929), Cultural theorist.

Reason 39

You'll Become An Unpaid Employee of the Toy Industry

Although the above quote holds some truth, there is another maltreated group: parents who have to put these toys together.

When you have children, you will discover that one of the least pleasant experiences is taking them to a toy store. Maybe it's because kids go into sensory overload. You will hear more crying in toy stores than in a dentist's office.

And after surviving the toy store adventure, you'll get home and realize your job has just begun. Toy companies no longer make toys. They make the parts. Parents make the toys.

When you see, *"Some Assembly Required,"* you can anticipate spending hours putting the thing together. The word "some" obviously has a different meaning to toy manufactures than it does for the rest of the population.

If you buy a toy that just says *"Assembly Required,"* you have signed on for a new career.

Toys used to come completely assembled. All you had to do was take them out of the box and watch your children have fun. This is no longer true, thanks to giant retailers such as Toys R Us and Walmart, who want to fit as many toys as possible on their shelves.

Toy companies put unassembled pieces into the smallest box possible, and parents get stuck spending hours trying to assemble them.

There should be a law that says if a toy is made for a four year old child, then a four year old child should be able to put it together.

Most toys require an engineering degree to be assembled — that is if you can understand the directions, which are usually written by someone from another planet.

And toy companies have pushed it even further. Not only will you have to put the toy together, you'll have to decipher a code for putting decals on—decals that are too small for an adult's hands and too confusing for a child's mind.

Once-upon-a-time Christmas morning was for watching children play with their toys. No longer! After weeks of shopping, decorating and cooking, you'll be spending most of Christmas day putting toys together.

If you're a Christmas Eve Santa, and like to have everything put together and under the Christmas tree when your children wake up and take that first peek, you'd better start early. While the toy industry is enjoying Christmas Eve parties and counting their profits, you'll be working overtime on their job—with no pay.

It won't take long before you start resenting a toy industry that has coerced an unwilling source of free labor: Parents.

Toys used to be for children to play with. Now they're for parents to put together, while your child anxiously asks, over and over, "Is it done yet?"

And of course, the day after Christmas will be spent standing in outrageously long lines, bringing back the toys that didn't have all the parts.

"Accidents will occur in the best regulated families"
Charles Dickens (1812-70), English novelist.

Reason 40
Injuries

Injuries are very much a part of a child's life, but injuries take on a whole new meaning when it's your child. And the meaning is fear.

I've seen a doctor's hands shaking while bandaging his son's bleeding, but not badly wounded, leg. He was a leading eye surgeon, with steady hands, who was not upset by the sight of blood, until it was his child's blood!

I'm not a squeamish person. When I was a kid I ripped my arm open, almost down to the bone. I simply wrapped a dish towel around it, and had my friend take me home on the handle bars of his bicycle. It didn't faze me, but my mother almost passed-out when she saw it.

Growing up, I skinned my knees so many times that the concrete in the alley behind my home was wearing thin. But the first time my 3rd grade son came in the door with his knee bleeding and the skin all mangled, my knees were shaking.

The slightest injury takes on a whole new meaning when it's your child. No matter how brave or strong you are, when you see your child hurt, you'll turn into milk-toast.

Risk is in front of kids at almost every turn as they journey through life's obstacle course. By nature or innocence they don't recognize it. They charge through life with reckless abandon. But for inches, luck, and angels, injuries are unavoidable.

The primary source of transportation for kids, outside of walking, is: bicycling, skateboarding, and roller-blading. With the ever increasing number of cars in this country, our kids have little room to play. And with all the incapable, aggressive and medicated drivers on the road, our children are at constant risk.

From the moment you let go of their hand, kids are walking hand-in-hand with danger.

Then they reach the driving age! Now the dangers magnify. That bone-chilling call from the police or hospital that you hope will never happen — well, it may. If it does, you better believe in God or some higher power, because it will be the scariest experience in your life, and you are going to feel totally helpless.

If your child has to undergo emergency surgery, you'll wish they could put you under anesthesia as well. Anesthesia would put you out of the agony of waiting, not knowing if your son or daughter will live or die, if he or she will ever walk again, or see again, or if your son or daughter will be disfigured for life.

It's like all the fears you've ever had in your life, plus all your worst nightmares, put together.

Kids today also have the additional horrors from guns. Today's version of a "*punch-in-the-nose*" can just as easily be a bullet in the head.

As we now know, no child, no matter where he or she lives, is safe from these new dangers. And no parent, no matter how they try to protect their child, can feel safe that tragedy won't befall their child.

On life's stress-o-meter there are many events that get high numbers for the amount of anxiety they cause, and the harmful effects they have on us physically and emotionally.

Your child's injuries will send that number through the roof! Isn't your stress-o-meter already high enough?

For statistical information visit www.50reasons.com

"There is always inequity in life. Some men are killed in a war and some men are wounded, and some men never leave the country. . Life is unfair."

John F. Kennedy (1917-63), U.S. president.

Reason 41

Down Syndrome, Autism, Etc.

What if? Nobody plans this twist of fate, but it happens. Having a child with a serious disability or illness is every expectant parent's worst thought. It is one of life's seeming inequities that will alter your life forever.

It's hard to understand why so many children start off life with such exceptional challenges. Even with all our medical advances, we seem to be making very little progress in preventing them. In fact, disorders like Autism, which was something I never heard about when I was growing up, is relatively common among our children today.

As an exceptional child's parent, you will have extraordinary demands and challenges as well. You will have to learn unique parenting skills.

Throughout your child's life you will have to do research, seek out qualified teachers and therapists, and demand adequate support services for your child.

Living with an exceptional child, accepting the challenges, and fulfilling these demands, can make you a better person — but it can also break you.

Emotionally and physically you'll have all the challenges of parenting, but it will be in a world in which few of your peers can relate.

Even family and friends may shy away from you and avoid the usual gab sessions about their kids and the stages they are going through. These daily interactions help maintain a parental equilibrium.

The support system that most parents take for granted will not be there for you, or at least it will not be easily accessible.

Should this twist of fate await you, your world will never be the same. With these afflictions go all your hopes and dreams, and the hopes and dreams you had for your child.

While no one can truly prepare for this possibility, you should at least considered it.

And as a parent of an exceptional child, your responsibilities won't end when he or she reaches 18 or 21 years of age. Your responsibility will continue throughout your life.

Possibly the most difficult part of having an exceptional child is worrying about how their life will be when you are no longer here to care for them.

What if? Are you capable of this lifelong commitment?

"Nothing has a stronger influence psychologically on their children than the unlived life of the parent."

Carl Jung (1875-1961), Swiss psychiatrist.

Reason 42

You Haven't Lived Your Life Yet

We tend to move too fast and too young into starting a family. Around our thirties or forties, we realize we never lived our own life. So then we start making all kinds of changes.

Those of us in this age group are changing families, careers, houses and spouses at an unprecedented rate.

For the most part, the first eighteen years of our lives are directed for us, primarily by parents and the educational system. Most of our activities are chosen by, or approved by, someone else. It's our life, but it's strongly influenced by others.

Obtaining a higher education can prolong this until our late twenties.

We usually emerge from these years with a lot of indoctrination and some knowledge — but little wisdom. We're only a fraction of the person we are capable of being.

This can be a time of great self discovery, moving from a black & white world into one of living color.

Whenever you become independent, whether it's after high school or graduate school, is a good time for worldly experiences. A time to live *your* life!

Beginning a family, committing to an occupation, or choosing a career before experiencing some variety in life can lead to years of doing something that brings frustration, stress, unhappiness and unfulfillment.

Consider moving away from your hometown, taking up residence in another state, traveling, or visiting another country.

You can learn more about the world and about yourself in one year of traveling than in twenty years of schooling. Traveling expands your awareness of different people, which will expand your knowledge of yourself.

You can always return to your safe corner of the world, but when you do, you will have a better understanding of the world.

However you chose to live your life, before starting a family is a good time to take some risk, to take a shot at some of the things you dream about. If you fall and skin your knees, it's OK. You will learn balance, and with that — wisdom.

You only have yourself to take care of now, and that's pretty easy to do. Taking care of a family — that's hard. Once you have a child, taking a shot at your dreams comes with a much greater risk, because the stakes are so much higher.

If you don't live your life to its fullest before you start a family, you may never get another chance.

You will never have this combination of individual freedom, youthful exuberance, unlimited potential and energy, with plenty of time to rebuild if things don't work out.

Before having children is your time to reach for the sky, and if you fall short, play in the stars.

Discover yourself and pursue your dreams?

Or!

Change diapers filled with guacamole and beans?

"We often speak of love when we really should be speaking of the drive to dominate or to master..."

Thomas Szasz (b.1920), Author.

Reason 43

You Believe In Tough Love

Often ideas or opinions are given an identifying word or phrase that becomes a slogan. That's what happened as a result of the TOUGHLOVE books. (The authors used this as a single word to identify this concept.)

Many parents describe hitting and other questionable actions as *tough love*. Whether or not that's what the authors intended, the term has become a catch phrase and is often used by parents to hide behind.

To begin with, *tough* is an adjective that shouldn't go in front of the word *love,* especially when it applies to our children. It diminishes the word. Tough *parenting* would make more sense.

Tough love is often as misleading and confusing to parents as it is to children.

When my children were acting-out in ways I disapproved of, tough love became an attractive alternative, because I was frustrated, angry, and in denial as to how my role as a parent played into my children's behavior.

So I contacted the local chapter of TOUGHLOVE, requested information and read the book. But right from the beginning the theory seemed old and outdated, blaming the impact of the 1960's &

1970's for *"much of the unruly behavior experienced in today's families."*

In today's hectic world, we give our kids very little of our time. During what little time we do give, we place many demands on them. Then, when our children resort to acting-out to get our attention, we give them tough love, by sending them to boot-camps or scare factories.

These forms of tough love may appear to work, but they probably cause more problems than they solve. Tough love is like communism: On paper it looks good — getting everyone marching in step to the same beat (in fear of course), but in practice it kills the human spirit.

While some of the ideas advocated in TOUGHLOVE are valid, too often the generic term, *tough love,* is used to defend parental unaccountably, or worse, to justify abusive parenting.

It has become too easy for parents to excuse their own inappropriate behavior under the disguise of tough love.

When I was a child, my mother's form of tough love was screaming at me and shaking me; my father's form was hollering and hitting. They would often tell me it was because they loved me. They both said, *"some day you'll understand."*

Well, that some day came — and I understood completely. I understand that they resorted to the easiest and most primitive way of dealing with challenging situations.

Because they were unskilled in parenting and refused to get counseling, I had to take years of physical and emotional abuse. Their belief in tough love is what gave them the green light.

Tough love in the wrong hands hurts — physically and emotionally, and often leaves permanent scares.

Like many parents, I'm guilty of getting caught up in feeling that my children don't show me love. I also *assumed* that they knew how much I love them.

With the help of counseling, I began to realize that my children needed more love. They needed it expressed more often, and in more positive ways. As I acknowledged this, their destructive behavior began to change for the better.

One example is when my younger son would often say "I don't care," when he would get in trouble, or when I scolded him. While in a program called *Teen Care*, with our counselor sitting-in, he said it again.

I began explaining why he had to care, and that it was important for his life today and in the future, when the counselor stopped me.

She said, "Look at your son. Don't you hear what he is *trying* to say?"

I said, "Yes! He's saying he doesn't care."

She explained to me how very often kids don't know how to express their feelings, and that what he was trying to say was that he was scared and hurting.

She suggested that every time he says he doesn't care, I change the words in my mind (for you computer users, like creating a macro) so that when he said, *"I don't care,"* I heard *"Dad, I'm scared and feeling overwhelmed."*

It helped me stop for a moment, and not immediately get frustrated trying to tell him why he must care. Once I played the macro in my mind, I would respond to a scared child with love, instead of responding to a defiant child with indignation.

It helped me look at the situation differently, and he began responding differently.

When I began reacting with love and understanding, he began coming to me to discuss the situation more openly, providing me an opportunity to then give him guidance.

It has been so effective that he now catches himself when he says *"I don't care."* He realizes that is not what he really means, and is able to resolve many issues within himself.

Isn't that what all parents strive for? That their children will understand what causes problems in their life, and alter the behavior on their own. It didn't take tough love. It took more love.

If you are going to have kids, consider this novel approach: try replacing tough love with unconditional love. This may be more challenging and require more accountability, dedication, and creativity on your part, but some day your children will thank you for it.

Love — pure unadulterated love — can accomplish the miraculous!

"Children have never been very good at listening to their elders, but they have never failed to imitate them."

James Baldwin (1924-87), Author.

Reason 44

You're A *"Do As I Say — Not As I Do"* Person

When I was younger I looked forward to the day when I was granted *parental privilege* — the ability to tell my kids, "don't holler" while I yell at them. To be able to send them off to church while I sit at home. And of course to tell them not to curse, while my language is peppered with off-color words and expressions.

I was looking forward to the day when I gave the orders but didn't have to follow them. Like my parents, I wanted to mandate, not model. And like most parents, I was good at seeing misbehavior in my children, while I overlooked my own shortcomings. It was easier setting my kids straight than setting myself straight.

But then I began seeing how my behavior was being emulated by my kids, just as clearly as I could see how I was emulating some of the negative behaviors of my parents.

I had to acknowledge the fact that my actions and behavior, whether subtle or overt, were not only setting examples for my children, but becoming a part of their personalities.

Like so many other situations, I was again reminded that this is a different age from when I grew up. We are more enlightened today than our parents were, just as they were more enlightened than their parents.

In spite of our human frailties, we continue to evolve. With our evolution comes new understandings and higher responsibilities.

Our challenges as parents are far greater in today's world. Your children will be less inclined to listen to you, and more likely to question you.

"Do as I say, not as I do" never really worked. It was just easy parenting, and another way parents pass on family dysfunction.

Kids listen to your words sacrilegiously, but follow your example religiously. Tell your children not to steal, while you take things from work, and they'll have sticky fingers. Tell them to drive slowly, while you drive fast, and they'll have lead feet.

Tell your children not to quit, that they can achieve their goals, while you get a divorce, failing to uphold your vows. And when the going gets tough they'll likely throw the towel in.

I know this flies in the face of what science is trying to convince us of — that it's all in the genes. But being a *do as I say, not as I do* person myself, I've seen that my examples molded my children. As I changed my actions, they changed their behavior. It didn't take gene therapy, it took family therapy.

So take some unscientific advise. If you're a *do as I say, not as I do* person, keep your genes in your pants. Or at least learn to take your own advice.

"The art of life is the art of avoiding pain; and he is the best pilot, who steers clearest of the rocks and shoals with which it is beset."

Thomas Jefferson (1743-1826), U.S. president

Reason 45

They Will Break Your Heart

Heartache has many forms. With children you will likely experience them all. When you have children, they possess your heart. With each new faze of a child's life comes ample opportunity for your heart to be broken. If their lives crumble, so does your heart. There's little you can do about it.

When your child comes home crying because he or she was made fun of at school, wasn't picked to play on the team, or was emotionally degraded with a cruelty that only another child can do, you not only see the pain on his or her face, you feel it in your heart.

A child's heartache is a parent's heart-break.

I remember my son's first week of school. His mother and I talked about it as a happy and exciting event. He believed us. He had a bounce in his little step when I dropped him off the first day. But before long, he was coming home scared and upset because one of the boys was bullying him.

Along with the anger I felt, my heart ached for him. I knew he had many years of bullies ahead of him, and as a sensitive boy he was going to have it tough. The pain, the joy, the sorrow and all the other emotions that his little heart would feel, would be felt by me as well.

Like most of us, by the time I was in my 20's, I had experienced heartache on a few fronts. I believed that I had already weathered the worst heartache possible — that of a lost love. It may have been *puppy love*, but its ending was quite painful.

I thought then that I had a strong heart — one that no one could ever break again. And the real sensitive places within my heart became *closed* to visitors.

But the day my first son was born, the closed sign was forever removed. And like children will do, he discovered places within my heart that I never knew existed.

Only the coldest hearts among us can remain numb to the pain that a child inevitably will bring. Unfortunately, such a heart also freezes out the warmth, pleasure and joy of having a child, and will more than likely leave the child with a frostbitten heart as well.

When my son was seven years old he had to have surgery. On the big day, he was trying to act bravely. Like a little trouper he marched into the hospital, his small fingers holding my hand like it was his favorite security blanket on a stormy night. When he bravely let go and was wheeled off to the operating room, I realized just how fragile my heart was when it pertained to my children.

In the waiting room I worried, and prayed, and realized how my children completely occupied my heart. If anything happened to either one of them, the emptiness would be more than I could bare. It was scary to be so vulnerable.

The operation went fine. I thanked God and the surgeon repeatedly. However, I was keenly aware of

"What if?" and the many families who are on the heartbreaking side of that question every day.

From the moment your child is born you'll give them your heart completely. Not only does it feel safe, it's the natural and noble thing to do. But when you give your heart so freely, it's much easier for it to become broken completely.

A baby fills your heart with smiles, nibbles and dribbles. But a teenager drains it with why's, lies and outcries.

As my children got older, I began to expect more love and consideration from them, but I discovered that a teenager's world is self-centered. With the best of intentions, I often did things for my sons, only to have them tell me that they didn't care.

I'd work hard to give them some material thing they wanted, and then watched it get broken and discarded. I put my heart into making their school lunch, and because they were mad at me, watch them throw it down the gutter.

Anger was often my reaction, but heartache was always what I felt.

I often got blamed for everything bad that happened to them. When I did not give-in to what they wanted, they told how much they hated me, saying that they wished I wasn't even their father.

Whether they meant it or not, hearing these words hurt. The heart is a very emotional organ which is not guided by logic.

The teenage years have been turbulent. I've had to make many difficult parenting decisions, and put them into practice. These actions have often been greeted with a barrage of obscenities.

Having struggled for so many years to give my children the things they *wanted*, it was extremely hurtful being called an "ass-hole" because I was now giving them what they *needed*.

As a child, my father would have beaten me to a bloody mess for talking to him like that. That my sons would talk to me like that left my heart feeling like a bloody mess.

There are times when fate seems to work against the most well-meaning parent. I didn't choose for them to get into trouble right before Father's Day. But my job as a father required that my children suffer the consequences as a result of their actions, and I did my job.

So on the one day to celebrate fathers and the good things they do, a day that makes a year's worth of trials and tribulations seem like a good deal, I sat waiting for a Father's Day card or some other acknowledgment that never came.

No angioplasty or open-heart surgery can fix this kind of broken heart.

From the cradle to college, the landscape is littered with heart-breaking experiences.

If there is wisdom in the opening quote by Thomas Jefferson, that, *"The art of life is the art of avoiding pain,"* then you should steer clear of having children, because they will surely break your heart.

"I have always thought that one man of tolerable abilities may work great changes, and accomplish great affairs among mankind, if he first forms a good plan..."

Benjamin Franklin (1706-90), U.S. statesman, writer.

Reason 46

You Don't Have A Family Plan

Starting a family is probably the most life-altering decision you'll ever make. Most of us don't realize that running a family is as challenging as running a business. I've done both, but I'll admit I put more time into my business plan than my family plan.

When starting a business, a business plan is a necessity. But when starting a family, a family plan is usually neglected.

A business plan is essential because it requires you to be extremely thorough when starting and thinking through a business. Financial requirements, goals, and a game-plan to achieve those goals are a vital part of it. For any business plan to be taken seriously, it must anticipate obstacles as well.

A family plan is not just how many children you want. Many family plans are little more than baptisms, bar mitzvahs and birthdays.

The key to a family plan is spending time considering all of the ramifications of starting a family. Along with financial responsibilities, a family plan must place emotional needs high on the scale, because they're the life-blood of a healthy or "dis-eased" family.

Like a business plan, a family plan must consider the down-side in a logical and non-emotional way.

Talk with friends and family about the pitfalls of having kids. Don't just ask what it's like having children. Be specific about **the down-side** of having kids, including the unexpected problems. There's a good chance you'll experience similar situations.

Each family may have unique circumstances, beliefs, and goals, but taking the time to think ahead, anticipate, and plan, will benefit everyone.

Think it out thoroughly, from A to Z. The more you plan, the better off you'll be.

Abortion - Ever or Never?

Baby-sitters - Who will you trust? $(costs)

College - You have to start planning for this from birth. $$$$

Daycare - Yes or no? When and why? How long? $$$

Entertainment - Movies, sporting events, parties, etc. $$

Food - Who shops? Who cooks? Eating out? Lots of $$$

Graduations - And birthdays, religious celebrations, etc. $$

Housing - Apartment or House? Rent or buy? $$$$

Inoculations - Which ones? How safe? Circumcise or not?

Job-sharing - Who does what? Housework is real work!

K tru 12 - Homework, parent teacher nights, school trips.

Lessons - Dance, music, etc. A lot of chauffeuring! $$

Money - How much do you earn? How much will you need?

Nurturing - Very important at all ages, but easily neglected.

Occupations - Who, what, when & where?

Pots & pans - And other necessities for a home. $$

Quality of schools - Very important. Can be costly. $$$

Religion - Can cause insurmountable problems. Discuss it!

Sickness - Throws a monkey wrench into the best plan.

Teenage years - Proms, cars, sex, drugs and Rap!

Unfaithfulness - It happens! Throw the towel in or seek help

Vacations - All families need and deserve them. $$

Working parents - Who's watching the kids?

X-spouse - Now what?

Yule-tide celebrations - Shopping, cooking and lots of $$$.

Zero-hour - Think now or forever hold your peace.

Starting a business doesn't guarantee success, security or prosperity. But a business plan can help. Likewise, starting a family doesn't guarantee fulfillment, stability, or happiness. But a family plan can help.

Starting a business without a business plan is like driving at night without headlights. Starting a family without a family plan is like putting your child in that car.

If you don't have time to put together a family plan, you don't have time for a family.

"The experience and behavior that gets labeled schizophrenic is a special strategy that a person invents in order to live in an unlivable situation."

R.D. Laing (1927 - 1989), British psychiatrist, Author.

Reason 47

Mental Illness (Emotional Dis-Ease)

It was so called "mental illness" that took my wife and the mother of my children from our lives. This is a fate that at times seems worse than loss by death.

Schizophrenia, multiple personality disorder, and manic/depressive were just some of the diagnoses. No matter what the diagnoses, the treatment was always the same — very strong and debilitating drugs, with all kinds of negative side effects.

My children, like all children, love their mother very much. It has been very hard for them to watch her deteriorate. It has been equally hard watching a woman I care about suffering such a fate.

Even though we're divorced and I received full custody of our sons, she remained a close part of our lives. I've been exposed to, and have learned more about, mental illness than I ever wanted to.

I have some very strong **opinions** about the conditions labeled as mental illness. They are based on my own experiences and research. I must tell you right up front, they're contrary to what most, but not all, in the psychiatric industry believe.

Often, what is labeled "mental illness," is not a disease of the brain, and is not genetic. Mental illness has more to do with the emotions than it does with the brain.

A confused or irrational mind is often the result of abused or neglected emotions. Parents are often the primary cause, either directly or indirectly, of the emotional breakdown that results in their children. Therefore, parents can do a lot to prevent it.

Having a spouse with a mental illness was extremely difficult, hard to understand, and heartbreaking. But nothing will challenge you as a parent like having a child diagnosed with a mental illness.

No parent wants to see his or her child suffering such an affliction. However, mental illness is far more prevalent than you may be aware, because it's still the least talked about family secret.

I've seen and experienced the devastating effects mental illness (emotional dis-ease) has on a family. I've seen how ineffective, and often more damaging, the primary method of treatment (very strong mind-altering drugs) are.

The psychiatric and drug industries have provided emotional candy for parents with the "chemical imbalance" theory. This prevailing theory suggests drugs as the answer for almost every emotional condition. This often prevents real, and lasting, emotional healing to take place.

Peter R. Breggin, M.D., a Harvard-educated Psychiatrist, former teaching fellow at Harvard Medical School, and author of the best selling book *Toxic Psychiatry*, (a MUST read if you're ever considering drugging your child) has done extensive research on the drugs, and their terrible side effects, the psychiatric industry pushes to cure "mental illness".

According to Dr. Breggin, *"A growing body of psychological research confirms the obvious—that troubled families raise a high percentage of troubled children, who go on to be troubled adults."*

Many children that are diagnosed with a "mental illness" are really suffering from emotional distress. But accepting that truth requires parents to take some responsibility for the situation. And even harder, to change the situation and themselves.

My ex-wife grew up in a family bleeding with dysfunction. She was subjected to divorce, abandonment, and sexual abuse from a very young age. As an extremely sensitive child, she lived an emotionally tortured life.

When she started showing signs of emotional distress it was labeled a "chemical imbalance." But although it was her family that was out of balance, *she* was locked away in a mental institution and drugged.

Just like smoking rots the lungs, and alcohol abuse destroys the liver, physical and psychological abuse will shatter the emotions, as what happened in her case.

Chemical imbalance = parent absolution. And it almost always results in the child being drugged.

Over the years my ex-wife has repeatedly sought help from the psychiatric profession. Without exception, every psychiatrist recommended strong drugs, some so toxic that monthly blood tests were required.

I've been a first hand witness to the damage long term use of these drugs can cause.

In my own family, years of physical beatings and verbal abuse led to years of depression so deep all I wanted to do was to die.

Confronting my parents with the damage they inflicted, although met with their denial, was the beginning of the end of my depression. With therapy, and *without* drugs, depression has been eradicated from my life.

In our society today, children with a so-called "mental illness," although the most fragile, are often the most mistreated.

The more sensitive the child, the more destructive the experience will be. The way many children with emotional dis-ease are being treated is downright cruel.

They are being locked away, strapped down, drugged, sexually abused, and sometimes even suffocated to silence them. The conditions and practices at many psychiatric hospitals are deplorable.

Primary reasons for emotional dis-ease in children stem from parents not healing their own emotional wounds, and thus creating an unstable, undependable and unlivable environment that their children are forced to live. But parents have a ready and willing collaborator for their denial.

According to Dr. Breggin, *"Modern psychiatry pushes us in one direction—toward blaming the victim and exonerating the adult authorities. It's the easy way out for all of the adults, including the child abuser; but it's a disaster for the child."*

Since the damage had already been done to my wife, and those that caused it had long since washed their hands in the muddy waters of denial, I trusted the medical profession and put a lot of faith in their drugs.

My children and I got our hopes up with each new drug the psychiatric and pharmaceutical industry touted as a miracle drug. Ever so short progress was *always* followed by a more serious breakdown.

What the psychiatrists called progress, my children and I saw as a slow moving, slow thinking, tired mother, unable to do the things she so wanted to do.

When she would come home from the hospital she was little more than a zombie because of the drugs injected into her.

We watched a loving, but troubled, woman and mother slowly have any remaining joy in life smothered out of her.

At best, medicine is a crutch to provide temporary support for the damaged emotions, not a cure.

If you break your leg support is needed to take the pressure off while the bone heals. But you wouldn't rely on the crutch as a permanent solution.

Much like a broken leg needs good physical therapy to heal and become strong again, the emotions also need good therapy to heal and become whole again.

Treating the brain with drugs instead of treating the emotions with understanding is putting the cart before the horse.

Drugging the brain does little, if anything, to heal the emotions. But healing the emotions does a lot, if not everything, in healing a troubled mind.

To use a computer analogy: the brain is the hardware, the emotions are the software. If the brain isn't functioning, it's more than likely a software problem.

Even if there is only a slight chance that a parents' role plays a part in the emotional and mental health of their child, isn't it worth exploring before you decide to have children?

Denial in many parents is intense when it comes to this subject. But there can be no denying the pain and anguish when mental illness manifests in your child.

Mental illness can turn parenting into a nightmare. All the denial in the world will not help your children, or the troubled adults they turn into.

Those street people you see in tattered clothes, begging for money, and sleeping over manholes, are not the lazy low-life's they've been portrayed as. Most of them are suffering from mental illness (emotional dis-ease). But all of them are somebody's child.

For more information on Mental Illness go to www.50reasons.com

"Most American children suffer too much mother and too little father."

Gloria Steinem, (b 1934), Feminist writer

Reason 48

You'll End Up A Father Without A Child

You may be blissfully in love with your wife when you have a child, but the odds are it will not stay that way. When relationships start to fall apart between a husband and wife, this can get ugly.

We never think we will be a statistic, but it's a fact that about 60% of all marriages will end in divorce.

When a marriage with children deteriorates, the kids are often used as a trump card, and the woman almost always holds the winning hand. And with that hand goes your children, the house, and a good chunk of your paycheck.

It's estimated that there are about 12 million fathers in the United States living without their children. I'm in a very small minority of divorced fathers with sole custody of their children. But as was revealed in Reason 47, there were some serious issues and extreme circumstances in my unusual case.

Since I had to be both dad and mom for my boys, I felt I owed it to them to better learn about and understand the role of a mother. I wanted to see the world through a woman's eyes, especially when it pertained to parenting and nurturing, so I started hanging out with moms.

Before long I was *clipping* coupons, *sorting* the laundry, and *rinsing* the dishes before putting them in the dishwasher.

Even worse, drinking beer and talking about sports got replaced with sipping herbal tea and listening to gossip - which proves the sacrifices a man is willing to make for his kids!

I'll admit that over time I've become "estrogen'ized." But I still have that dreaded *testosterone* flowing through my veins. And since this reason is being written for guys, I'm going to let the facts spill out like beer from a freshly taped keg, without all the frothy political correctness being poured down your throats.

Even though society is slowly beginning to acknowledge the importance of a father in a child's life, our courts are still far behind. Your soon-to-be ex-wife will have you by the balls! Not only will she know it, she won't hesitate to squeeze, and bring you to your knees.

No matter how good of a father you are, the mother will almost certainly win custody. Your ex will then make most of the decisions in your children's lives, often without even consulting you.

What you consider important for their well-being and essential in their upbringing, will often be viewed as meddling.

Contrary to the never ending and overblown media reports, most fathers do their best to physically, emotionally and financially support their children. Regardless of that fact, fathers routinely get beat up in the court of law, and in the court of public opinion. Men's grievances often go unheard and most people don't care about them.

If an extra-marital affair is the cause of the breakup, and this is not unlikely, your children's *tooth-fairy* will become your *Wicked Witch of the West.*

Many women **use** the little munchkins, no matter how hurtful, cruel and unfair, to get what they want. And while the house will likely fall in her lap, the mortgage will crush *you*.

If it's your wife who's having the affair, your broken heart, shattered emotions and crumbling world will matter little in her quest for custody.

Heaven forbid if it's you having the affair! Castration, tar and feathering, and public ridicule will likely be too lenient to satisfy her.

When there are children involved in a divorce, women need to start behaving like mothers instead of ex-lovers. But don't hold your breath for that.

The future that may await you, as it does many fathers, is: Being the target of choice for blame and shame by your ex to your kids. Feeling responsible for the bad things that happen in your children's lives, but being unable to share in the good. Ending up as little more than a source of money, whether or not you agree with how it's being spent.

And if you fall on hard times, getting labeled a *deadbeat dad*, hauled into court, humiliated and dishonored. For what? To see your kids once in a while, have little say in their daily lives, remain powerless on the sideline.

In just one generation, men have reinvented fatherhood by embracing a more involved role in their children's lives. Yet fathers are still devalued in divorce proceedings, and left feeling *non-essential* in raising their children.

Statistically speaking, you're likely to become one of the millions of fathers who works and sleeps and works, without complaining, to provide for the children you see part-time, but love full-time. Realistically speaking, you're likely to end up a father without a child.

"What I have absolutely no sympathy with is the man who seeks, for his own profit, to exploit the weaknesses of those who are unable to help themselves and then to fasten some moral superscription upon it."

Malcolm Lowry (1909-57), British novelist

Reason 49

You're An Emotional Junk Food Junkie

Here's a simple test to see if you're an emotional junk food junkie: Do you watch Jerry Springer, Maury Povich, Montel Williams, or any of the other Trash TV shows?

They don't have to be the above mentioned national ones. They can be your local sleaze and titillation shows. Any and all of them must be included.

If you're consuming any of these type shows regularly, you're an emotional junk food junkie. Watching them daily can cause emotional malnutrition.

I know this sounds a bit bold, but stick with me on this. At worst, it's food for thought. You'll benefit from this one with, or without children.

These type shows are junk food for your emotions. A diet of this noxious entertainment eventually affects how one thinks and feels.

As junk food has been the biggest contributor to the fattening of America, this type of emotional junk food is responsible for the dumbing of America — emotionally and intellectually.

As with all hollow calories, we just keep wanting more. As a result, even the so called "respectable" media are now serving up a daily menu of this type of shallow and intrusive fare.

We have become a society of emotional peeping Toms. Because we can watch from our living room doesn't make it any less distasteful.

We used to have traveling circuses that displayed the physically disfigured for people to gawk and make fun of. This ended only when society sickened from a diet of such hollow thrills.

Today, a few ringmasters display for profit a steady parade of emotionally disfigured people. These so called entertainers are profiting from humiliation and emotional brutality. They callously seek out and manipulate these unfortunate people.

Some of these ringleaders try to make you believe their shows are newsworthy or have educational value. But at best, these programs are like sweetened, over processed cereal with a few vitamins injected.

Watching emotionally disturbed people being sent into the arena to fight has become a pastime for many. As can be expected, those watching have already become desensitized. More emotional bleeding is needed to keep our attention. The sleaze pushers are competing with one another to provide it.

Seeing so much dysfunction being displayed makes it easy to see unhealthy behavior as normal. Even worse, viewing such extreme dysfunction feeds our own denial, allowing us to ignore the dysfunction within ourselves. "We're not as bad as them!"

To find these shows entertaining is sad. And for your children to see you consuming these toxic programs is irresponsible.

Children emulate parents far more than we realize, and for much longer into adulthood than we can imagine. They're aware of what their parents find entertaining, what they spend their time doing and where they get their information.

And children are always seeking a parent's attention. If they see that this type of behavior gets your attention, don't be surprised when they use it to get you to notice them.

By eliminating these programs from your diet you will see the world differently. It takes some strength not to get sucked into the titillating sound bites, to flick right by the *Springer's* and *Cheaters* without so much as a pause. But you'll be free of what grips so much of America today, and rightfully feel proud.

Why fill yourself with shallow calories when there are alternatives? It's much healthier to fill up on Oprah - packed with emotional nutrition.

There's no reason for this garbage to be on your TV. Many avenues of entertainment are stimulating — emotionally and intellectually, without pandering and exploiting people.

Raising children takes emotional strength, character and lots of positive influences. A steady intake of rotten images, ideas and behaviors will surely sicken ones spirit, and eventually leave the family emotionally malnourished.

Before you have kids, cut the emotional junk food out of your diet.

"Certainly the best works, and of greatest merit for the public, have proceeded from the unmarried, or childless..."

Francis Bacon (1561-1626), English philosopher.

Reason 50

You'll Be In Good Company

More people than ever are choosing to stay childfree. Outside of feeling somewhat discriminated against (flextime for parents, tax credits, school vouchers, childcare benefits), they are living happy, productive, enjoyable lives.

With more freedom, and more disposable income, more people are discovering that a life without children is *not* a life without joy and fulfillment.

People without children are sometimes viewed as being deprived, missing out on a blessing, or worse, selfish. For the most part it's just human nature, wanting others to be like the rest of us. There's comfort in conformity.

Every Mother's Day we celebrate those who bring babies into this world, and it's a wonderful day. But would it be such a special day if *childless* Anna Jarvis was too busy raising children to become the originator of the official Mother's Day?

Today, more people than ever are choosing to be childfree. According to U.S. Bureau of Census, in 1976, 35% of the women in America were childfree. In 1995 it was 42%. And the trend is continuing. It's becoming a more *childfree friendly* world.

Here's just a small list of individuals who've led, or are leading, rewarding and successful lives while remaining childfree. It's unknown whether being childfree was responsible for their great success. But as a parent, the one thing I do know, is they had a lot more time to devote to their life's pursuits, with a lot less worries and responsibilities.

Conformity was not for these childfree people from the past:

- George Washington - 1st President of the United States
- James Madison - 4th President of the United States
- Andrew Jackson - 7th President of the United States
- James K. Polk – 11th President of the United States
- Millard Fillmore - 13th President of the United States
- James Buchanan - 15th President of the United States
- Woodrow Wilson 28th President of the United States
- Ayn Rand – Author, Philosopher.
- Katherine Hepburn - Actress.
- Florence Nightingale - Nurse.
- Louis Armstrong - Musician
- Bill Wilson - Founder Alcoholics Anonymous
- Mark Twain - Author.
- Robert Goddard - Physicist, Father of Rocketry
- Emily Dickinson - Poet
- Jack Lord - Actor (Hawaii Five-O)
- Cecil Green - Co Founder of Texas Instruments
- Ludwig van Beethoven - Composer
- Leonardo Da Vinci - Artist, Renaissance Painter

- Sir Isaac Newton - Scientist, Mathematician
- Mother Teresa - Missionary, Nobel Peace Prize winner
- Joan of Arc - Biblical Saint
- Oliver Wendell Holmes - Justice of the Supreme Court
- Milton Hershey - Founder of Hershey Chocolate
- Luthur Vandross - Singer
- Francis Bacon - Philosopher, Statesman, Essayist
- Judith Resnick - Astronaut
- Rosa Parks - Civil Rights Activist
- Helen Keller - Author, Lecturer.
- Thomas Paine - Author, Political Theorist.
- Ray Kroc - Developer of McDonalds Restaurants
- Norman Rockwell - Painter
- Albert Schweitzer - Nobel Peace Prize Winner
- Jane Austen - Author, English Novelist.
- T. S. Eliot - Poet
- Raymond Burr - Actor (Perry Mason, Ironside)
- Frank Lausche - Governor of Ohio, U. S. Senator
- William Lyon Mackenzie King - Former Prime Minister of Canada
- Carolyn Jones - Actress (Morticia - Adams Family)
- Friedrich Nietzsche - Philosopher
- Copernicus - Scientist
- Lionel Hampton - Bandleader, Jazz Musician
- Orville & Wilber Wright - Aviators
- Sir Francis Drake - Explorer

- George Bernard Shaw - Nobel Prize Literature
- Kate Smith - Singer (God Bless America)
- Amelia Earhart - Aviator
- Dr. Seuss - Children's author.
- Plato - Philosopher

That's a pretty productive group of people! Their legacy was what they achieved with their own life, not their children's.

Conformity is not for these recent day childfree people (as of this writing) as well:

- Oprah Winfrey - TV host, Actress.
- Rita Rudner - Comedian.
- Dalai Lama - Tibetan Spiritual Leader
- Sheryl Crow – Musician
- Linda Evans – Actress.
- Maureen Dowd - Columnist
- Joe Kernan - Former Governor of Indiana
- Christopher Walken - Actor
- Gloria Gaynor - Singer
- Lou Reed - Musician
- Julie Kavner - Actress (Brenda in Rhoda, Voice of Marge Simpson)
- Sally Ride - Astronaut
- Helen Gurley Brown - Editor Cosmopolitan Magazine
- Bonnie Raitt - Singer, Songwriter.
- Helen Clark - Prime Minister of New Zealand
- George Clooney - Actor

- Diane Sawyer - TV News Anchor
- Jeff Goldblum - Actor
- Randy Travis - Country Singer
- Arsenio Hall - TV Personality
- David Souter - Supreme Court Justice
- Richard Simmons - Weight Loss Guru.
- Daryl Hannah - Actress
- Ann Coulter - Author, Columnist, Political Pundit
- Simon Cowell - TV Personality (American Idol)
- Jacqueline Bisset - Actress
- Gary Davis – Former Governor of California
- Marlo Thomas - Actress (That Girl)
- Julia Cameron - Author (The Artist Way)
- Delta Burke - Actress (Suzanne on Designing Woman)
- Bo Derek - Actress (10)
- Daryl Hall - Musician (Hall & Oates)
- Yanni - Composer/Musician.
- Quentin Tarantino - Movie Director (Pulp Fiction)
- Hugh Grant - Actor
- Elizabeth Dole - Senator, North Carolina
- Richard Chamberlain - Actor (Dr.Kildare, Shogun)
- Pat Buchanan - Political Personality
- Debbie Harry - Singer (Blondie)
- Jay Leno - TV host.
- Nancy Griffiths - Singer/ Songwriter (From a Distance)

- Bob Barker - Game Show Host (The Price is Right)
- Susan Helms - Space Shuttle Astronaut
- Brett Butler - Comedian
- Patricia Ireland - Former President of NOW
- Ralph Nader - Consumer Advocate
- Margaret Cho - Comedian
- Stevie Nicks - Singer, Songwriter (Fleetwood Mac)
- Steve Martin - Comedian, Actor.
- Alyssa Milano - Actress (Who's the Boss)
- Dolly Parton - Singer, Actress.
- Kathy Bates - Actress (Misery)
- Terry Gross - Public Radio Host (Fresh Air)
- Ellen Degeneres - Comedian
- Elton John - Musician, Singer
- Richard Lewis - Comedian
- Gloria Steinem - Feminist Activist
- Bill Maher – Comedian, Social commentator.

Those who've either chosen to be childfree, or who weren't able to have children, are faring quite well, even in their older ages.

The worst part seems to be *coming to grips* with being childless, especially for women in their 30's. But more people than ever are not just accepting being childless, but they are welcoming it. And there's an ever-growing support network for "childfrees."

In the not-so-distance past our lives consisted primarily of family and farm. We were far more dependent on a family for our existence and life's experiences.

Even though this is no longer true we still follow that path. There's a world of experiences within our reach today. Having children is not the litmus test on a life of value and virtue.

Oh, and there was one other person who left a pretty indelible mark on the world, despite not having children - Jesus.

"There's a time when you have to explain to your children why they're born, and it's a marvelous thing if you know the reason by then."

Hazel Scott (1920-81), U.S. entertainer.

Closing

Having children in this "daycare generation" is unlike anything in the past. Parents, for the most part, don't parent much anymore. Since we're just too busy, more and more parenting is being delegated to others.

Our children are being squeezed out of our busy lives, but nobody wants to admit it.

It's easy, especially in our warp-speed lifestyle, for life to be nothing more that fleeting events piled on top of one another. The importance and significance of these events in the lives of our children are often not realized until many years later.

Unfortunately, many of us, if not most, jump into parenting with little knowledge and less ability. As parents, this puts a lot of additional stress in our lives. For our children, it starts them out on a path of distress and dysfunction.

It's my hope that this book, in some little way, will help curb this tide.

Adults can play important roles in a child's life besides mother and father. A good aunt or uncle, by relation or friendship, can be as meaningful in a child's life as anyone. We've all had someone special in our childhood, outside of our parents.

In our "parenting-by-proxy" world, our children not only need positive role models, but active role models.

Hillary Clinton was right when she said that it takes a village to raise a child.

Unfortunately the villages in America today are filled with part-time parents, missing parents, single parents, and for too many children, no parents.

Creating biological offspring is not the only way to experience the love and affection that children offer. By expressing love, concern and compassion toward children, you will get it back tenfold.

You can be a trusted confidant to your sister or brother's children, or a friend's child, or a Godchild. Heaven knows they need all the help they can get.

You can be an angel for a child just by showing interest in what he or she does, listening to them when they talk, and caring about what they say.

It has been said that all women are mothers to all children, and all men fathers to all children. These are not just noble words, they're instinctive human traits.

Coaching, teaching, Big Brothers and Big Sisters, foster parenting, mentoring, working in daycare, or being a teacher's aide are just a few direct ways that can bring children into your life. You could even be a crossing guard or playground attendant.

There's no shortage of children or ways you can be involved with them.

From health care to education, from counseling services to recreation, our children remain a low priority. No vote, no voice. Politicians hear the loudest voices. You can be that voice advocating for children.

If you still choose to start a family, I hope you will consider taking parenting classes *before* having children. Don't wait until you're drowning in despair.

I can pretty much assure you that you need them. I can guarantee you'll benefit from them, and your children will be much better off because you did.

Your children's world will be filled with under-tows and rip-tides that can pull them away from you faster than you can imagine. Rescuing them once they've been swept away is far more difficult, and requires a lot more skills, than being alert and preventing it.

Parenting is the single most challenging job in the world. One that should not be entered into lightly.

Take it from one who knows:

Kids are great,
but once you have them, they seal your fate.

As babies they scream and cry,
and you can kiss your sex life good-bye.

The teenage years will be the worst,
when they discover alcohol to quench their thirst.

It used to be sex, drugs, and rock & roll for you,
well, now it's for them and there's nothing you can do.

So take some advice from me,
it's better to stay child free.

If I knew how painful raising kids was gonna be,
I would have gladly had a vasectomy!

To add your suggestions for "50 *More* Reasons Not To Have Kids"
go to www.50reasons.com

Free CD Order Form

Thank you for purchasing this book. I'd be pleased to send you an audio CD worth $19.95, at no charge to you except $3.95 for shipping & handling ($0.00 cost for MP3 download). This entertaining, informative, and funny CD highlights the *Reasons* in this book, and gives the stories behind them. It's especially good for college age kids on the go.

Please Print Clearly

Name:_____

Address:_____

City:_____

State:_____ Zip:_____

Phone: (_____)_____

E-Mail:_____

Please charge credit card:_____

Exp. Date:_____

Authorized Signature:_____

(Must have the above information)

Mail the completed order from with a check, money order, or cash for $3.95 for shipping & handling to:

JLS Publishing, 566 W. Woodland Ave. Springfield, PA 19064

or fax completed form to: 610-544-6555

or order on line at: **www.50reasons.com**

If you found this book helpful, informative, or enlightening, please tell your friends.
Thank You.

Printed in the United States
137798LV00002B/17/A